The Funny Thing

About Being

a

Widow?

By

Sandra E Manning

Thank you

First up, I would like to thank my wonderful husband Kenny for our fantastic life together. It was an adventure of the very best kind and I know that, despite some of the content here, you understand how hard I am trying to honour the legacy of your love, which is in no way diminished because of it.

'Until we can hold hands once more and make anything come true.'

Thank you to my family who each, in their own different ways, held me up when my own legs would not. Your unconditional love and support have left me forever in your debt and the fact that I am still here and seeking out new adventures is because of each and every one of you. I can only hope that your faith in me is justified.

To Jayne, my dear buddy and GOWNS collaborator, with whom I have shared a friendship since we lost our darling boys, which is quantified by depth rather than longevity, I can only say a huge thank you for helping me to make sense of all the traffic in my head in your calm organised way. GOWNS would never have been born without you and I thank you for all that you are.

To all those of you who have supported me, some of whom I have met personally, others only through your kind messages of support, I also extend my eternal gratitude.

A special thanks to the BHG, who never once doubted me when I doubted myself enough for the two of us, always, forever and a day, until half-past three.

Finally a word to my grandsons, whom I love beyond description, as did their precious granddad, who says hello from his red star. He wants you to both aim high and not be discouraged by the thought of failure because you are already a success.

Gentle breathing

By

Sandra E Manning in memory of our island.

Gentle breathing I must not break for it's five am and she's not awake

Gentle breathing gives way to sound of breaking waves and sunrise found

Gentle breathing is now all my own as I watch the gulls that haven't flown

Gentle breathing becomes less steady so I cast my line and make me ready

Breathing now is hard and fast a pelican reels by a fishing boat's mast

Breaths from the gulf caress my face whilst the sea birds gather for the start of the race

Gasping breaths dance in time with mine as a catfish wriggles on my tugging line

Sighing birds scrape the clear blue sky so it's time to release my hook and say goodbye

Gentle breathing and still you sleep, I will dry those tears that I know you'll weep

Contents

Introduction

On the 12th August 2014 at precisely 11.45 pm I became a widow and, as a consequence, the future founder of GOWNS, or Grieving Overwhelmed Widows Negotiating Stuff. Neither of these were destinations of choice.

At the risk of alienating those of you who have chosen this book in the hope of finding what might pass for advice on how to deal with the loss of a beloved partner or spouse, I should perhaps explain what you *won't* find beyond this introduction. I am not an expert on grief. In fact, any advice from me on how best to deal with the recognised *stages* of grief is likely to be as helpful as a gale-force wind might be to Donald Trump at an outdoor convention. Despite my best efforts to find them, I have no wise words to offer but those that I have chosen in place of those elusive pearls are, at least, an honest appraisal of my own negotiations from the point of my husband's cancer diagnosis to his subsequent death and beyond it. It is my sincere hope that, by sharing the minutiae of my own experiences in this way, I might not only help to illuminate some of the more obvious pitfalls, for the purposes of avoidance but also remind the reader that future happiness need not elude a bereaved spouse indefinitely.

If I readily admit to having no particular expertise in anything much, the one exception might be an ability to find the humour in situations where we would not ordinarily expect to find any. When I lost Kenny after a marriage that lasted for thirty-six years during which time we found a reason to laugh out loud on most days, a number of useful attributes abandoned me in droves. My common sense and ability to self-regulate were amongst the first casualties, but I remain ever thankful that my sense of humour, though battered and bruised, remained largely intact and the survival of which, is in no small way directly related to my own. Not that I was remotely amused when it came to the new title bestowed upon me at the point of Kenny's demise and, this time, given to me without any of the prior consent that had been necessary when I agreed to become his wife. The word widow derived from the Anglo-Saxon Widuwe is ugly in print, pronunciation and definition. Whilst it was true that I did have something of the *physical void* about me post mortem, becoming associated with a whole raft of negative stereotypes as an automatic consequence of becoming one is something that would have amused my late husband no end.

You need to look no further than the traditional pantomime to find, perhaps, one of the most easily recognised examples of this stereotyping in the character of Widow Twankey. Ironically, she is played by a man and is depicted as the rather hapless, and helpless, mother of Aladdin, upon whom she relies for survival.

It is yet another man, Barry Humphries CBE, whose alter ego Dame Edna Everage provides us with his caricature of the widow, this time in the form of a *global housewife and superstar* who famously lost her husband, Norm, to a *testicular murmur*. Then there are the differing types of widow, which include those who simply lose theirs to golf, football or the pub. Unlike the bereaved version, however, they can at least reclaim their absentee spouses on the 19th tee, at the close of play, or at chucking out time. Widow spiders mate only once and then ingest their partners, widows peaks are worn by vampires and, of course, my own particular favourite is the Merry Widow, of whom Oscar Wilde wrote in *The Importance of Being Earnest.*

'I hear her hair turned quite gold from grief'- I rest my case.

Whilst the title of Mrs reveals nothing about the state of the union a woman has entered into, only that she has, the title of widow, or indeed spinster for that matter conjures up images of sad and shrivelled up women who fall outside of the societal ideals we set for ourselves. It was quite surprising to me how other people changed towards me once I was no longer one half of a married couple. Some friends, for instance, were genuinely concerned about my continued fiscal well-being now that I no longer enjoyed the support of my husband, whilst others disappeared fairly quickly, following the bun fight after the funeral, for fear of finding out anything unfavourable. Then there were the wives who called their spouses closer to heel when in my company, clearly threatened by my new and solitary status, despite the fact that there had been no change in the values and morals which had guided me for most of my adult life. On more than one occasion I found it necessary to discreetly turn down an offer of help to relieve me of my *loneliness*. What follows is, essentially, an account of my diversions and detours as I struggled to face up to the pain of losing my husband whilst, at the same time, doing everything I could to overturn those stereotypical perceptions inflicted on me as a consequence. I was more successful in some of my negotiations than I was with others. Failing, quite spectacularly, in my bid to join my husband, during a time when my blood alcohol levels were likely to have been 37.5 per cent proof on most days, proved to be one of my more fortunate breaks. My inability to self-regulate extended to my finances, where I spent money as though I discovered that it did actually grow on trees, and my intention to write about the experiences of widows on dating sites gave me the perfect excuse to shag more unsuitable men than was good for me and call it research.

It has taken me over four years to write this book, not because I was slaving away trying to create something of literary merit which, when you consider that most of my early drafts were written in a state of alcoholic inebriation, was never very likely, but because I wanted it to be an accurate account of how I had faced, and dealt with, life as a Grieving Overwhelmed Widow Negotiating Stuff. In order to provide any legitimate comment on my negotiations, it was, of course, necessary for me to wait until I had experienced them fully and this takes place over a period of time which differs for each of us.

I have wondered many times throughout the last few years if I would ever again know of a life without the companion of grief in it, nowadays, I understand that the pursuit of a place in which you are said to be *over* your loss is pointless because no such place exists. This, of course, does not mean that we can't ever experience happiness again and, towards this end, we should aim to build for ourselves another existence around that core nucleus of grief to co-exist with it, rather than waiting for it to end. We are each the architects of our own future plans and the methods we employ to bring them to life are as unique to us as our fingerprints.

My own methods have included mistakes, bad decisions and, at times, behaviours of which I am not exactly proud, but I accept them all with gratitude for, without them, valuable lessons would certainly have been lost. Throughout all of my efforts, I always understood that making new connections was essential, not only to my survival, but in helping me to find a new niche in life which would give me back a sense of purpose and, unwittingly, it was my sense of humour which helped me to achieve this.

If meeting Jayne Benge, my partner in GOWNS, when I just happened to be online in the same place and time as she was, is the work of coincidence, which Jayne would say absolutely, that's exactly what it was, then so be it. I tend to believe that there are forces at work which influence these matters of *chance* more than we realise. Whatever the truth of this, Jayne and I would later learn that we shared an appreciation of humour, despite the reasons that had caused us to make our particular connection being no laughing matter. Once we discovered the very tangible benefits of using the power of laughter and applying it as a therapy, we were committed to finding ways in which to share this. The medium we chose was our GOWNS website, through which we also hoped to dispel all those unhelpful stereotypes around widows.

Did you know that laughter is?

An effective stress reliever - Muscles relax for up to 45 minutes after a good giggle.

It Boosts the immune system - As stress hormones decrease, and the production of infection-fighting antibodies and immune cells increase, this protects our bodies against illness. This is a huge benefit as GOWNS often suffer compromise to their immunity as a result of their loss and grief.

It releases endorphins – A natural *'feel-good'* chemical which can even act as a temporary form of pain relief and promotes a sense of well-being.

It increases blood flow - Blood vessels perform more efficiently. Increasing blood flow is a real advantage in the prevention of heart disease and cardiovascular problems.

It burns calories - OK, it might not be a substitute for the gym, but laughing for 10-15 minutes per day can burn up to 40 calories each time.

Our GOWNS website can be found online at www.gownsgroup.co.uk through which you can also access our YouTube channel and request membership of our closed group on Facebook, a place where our members can talk about the issues that are important to them in a safe and controlled environment and, of course, share the things that have given them cause to smile. Anyone interested in learning more about GOWNS and our Gigglefest workshops can send us an e-mail to: info@gownsgroup.co.uk where we will also be happy to answer any other questions that you might have.

'If you can learn to laugh again, so can you learn to live again' – Sandra Manning

Chapter one

The end of the beginning

The signs of change

"Can I have chicken nuggets and chips please, Grandma?" My three-year-old grandson's simple request for food, after an arduous nine-hour flight, was quickly followed by hysterical laughter as our people carrier drew up alongside the window of a toll booth on a central Floridian highway and not the *Drive-Thru* at McDonald's that the tired and hungry boy had clearly assumed it was. The discovery that he was evidently very familiar with the concept of fast food, despite my well-documented disapproval of it, caused me to deliver an expression in the direction of both his parents designed to convey my annoyance, though when I looked at the little fella's crumpled and confused features as we drove away from the toll booth empty-handed, I had to agree with my husband, Kenny, that a quick detour towards the golden arches of McDonald's was justified on this occasion.

This time the window delivered the goods and our gang of intrepid travellers were soon happily munching away on their food with, of course, one obvious exception who would have preferred to have eaten her own face than any form of fast food. At least Kenny seemed to be enjoying his burger: never a man with the largest of appetites, he was eating even less of late and I noticed that his gold wedding band, once a snug fit, now slid past his knuckle with ease. It was also true that the man affectionately known in the family as the Duracell bunny on account of his seemingly limitless reserves of energy was starting to tire more easily too. Whenever I suggested that he book himself an appointment with our GP for a quick check-up, Kenny would simply give me his adorable cheeky chappie grin and tell me that aside from being middle-aged, knackered and married to a certified raving lunatic that he was absolutely fine, an explanation I was only too willing to accept.

It was August 2013 and after an overnight pit stop in Orlando, the family headed south-west to our favourite place on the planet. The tiny island of Captiva was somewhere we had discovered quite by accident many years before –and - when we reached the bridge that straddled the San Carlos bay separating the islands of Sanibel and Captiva from mainland Florida, I was confident that our special place would soon work its magic and restore my husband to his former vibrant self. Even now, as I accept that my concerns for the state of my husband's health probably ran far deeper than I was prepared to acknowledge at the time, I certainly did not think that this would be the last time that Kenny would ever set foot on our beloved Captiva Island.

The diagnosis

On the 27th of December 2013, Kenny was handed a diagnosis of gastric cancer during an exploratory endoscopy carried out at our local hospital, though initially, he kept this information to himself.

After our return from Florida his deep and healthy-looking tan did little to camouflage the fact that he was anything but healthy. His appetite had continued to decline and, as a result, the pounds that he could ill afford to lose were melting away with alarming speed. He was spending most of his afternoons dozing in an armchair, and it was increasingly obvious that we needed to investigate the cause of his worsening symptoms. A week before Christmas Kenny made an appointment with our GP, who referred him to the hospital as a matter of urgency.

Christmas was a tense affair in our house that year. The tinsel glittered as usual and the fairy lights continued to shine, but our jocular life-sized karaoke Santa seemed to have suddenly acquired all the charisma of the grim reaper, though neither Kenny nor I vocalised our innermost fears concerning a possible diagnosis.

On the day of Kenny's appointment I sat in the hospital waiting room, with my gaze fixed firmly on the door behind which his procedure was taking place. Each time it opened, I forensically scanned the faces of the staff, searching for any clue as to my husband's fate. After a while, I suddenly became aware of a very strange sensation which felt like something was crawling all over my scalp, before it spread over the rest of my body, and was followed by an urge to be violently sick. I managed to persuade the contents of my stomach to remain in situ and, after what seemed to have been ages, but was probably only about half an hour, Kenny re-appeared flanked by two nurses with whom he was laughing and joking, as he did with almost everyone he met.

The knot in the pit of my stomach loosened ever so slightly: could the fact that my husband's cheeky grin was still very much intact possibly mean that we had landed ourselves a *get out of jail free* card? I noticed then that he was holding a white form which I tore from his grasp so that I could search it for clues as to his diagnosis. The results of his procedure seemed to indicate that he was suffering from the effects of a gastric ulcer. Kenny hugged and reassured me that he was absolutely fine, and we left the hospital as though we were walking on air, or at least one of us did.

Once we were back at home I wanted to relay the news of Kenny's diagnosis to a lot of people who quite frankly, like me were probably expecting to hear the worst, but Kenny was strangely reticent for me to do so. I assumed that this was because the high cost of phone calls was a regular bone of contention in our house, mainly due to my capacity to talk for long periods of time about nothing very much, and my careful husband lived in constant fear of becoming bankrupted by the phone bill. The afternoon passed much like any other. Kenny was dozing in his chair, a practice I expected he would dispense with once the ulcer had been treated and he was fully restored to his former Duracell charged self, when my sister and brother in law turned up unannounced, giving me the opportunity to share our good news at last. However, when I showed them the card from the hospital with the diagnosis written on it, their reactions were not at all what I had been expecting. My sister, Jacqueline, was nervously biting her bottom lip whilst Mark, my brother in law, appeared to be struggling to maintain his composure. Confused and more than a little scared by now, I asked Kenny what was going on and he came and sat down beside me before gently explaining that during the endoscopy it hadn't been a gastric ulcer that they had found but a large tumour situated in his stomach. Further tests would be necessary to confirm whether or not the tumour was malignant but, in the doctor's opinion, it was highly likely that it was.

I started to hear a kind of whooshing sound in my ears, something akin to the white noise of a radio or television, into which Kenny's words were slowly disappearing. Illogically, I decided that if I could remove myself from the source of this sound, then it might be possible to find my way back to the place I was in before I heard it. I bolted towards the back door and kept on running until my middle-aged knees, overburdened by middle-aged spread, simply refused to carry me further. I collapsed in a sobbing heap in the open field behind our house, with Jacqueline holding me tightly as I cried like I never had before.

This was, of course, precisely why Kenny had not been truthful about his diagnosis whilst we were still in the confines of the hospital. It would be easy to assume that this deception was cruel in that it allowed me to hope, where ultimately there was none to be had, but he was fully aware of how my past affected my ability to deal with news as devastating as this and, even now during the worst moment in his own life, his priority remained my protection and stands in testament to the man that he was.

My fear of those around me becoming ill has its origins in the health problems of my dear late mother. She had significant cardiac issues and endured up to fifteen major surgeries in her lifetime, some of which were ground-breaking and experimental, and were carried out by world-renowned surgeons at Saint Bartholomew's hospital in London. This involved long periods of separation for us as a family and, from about the age of ten years old, I was destined to spend a large part of my life in and around a hospital environment. My father worked overnight in the family business so it was I who called the ambulance and accompanied my mother to the hospital when problems arose, which as a minimum was at least twice a week. Even now, some fifty years later, the sound of wailing sirens and the flashing blue lights, that mirrored the colour of my mother's oxygen starved hands, are still as vivid in my mind as they were during the literally hundreds of times that I accompanied her to the hospital in the back of those ambulances.

My mother suffered from supraventricular tachycardia a condition which caused her heart to race dangerously in an abnormal rhythm, and the only way to rectify this in those days was to give her an electric shock to stop her heart and then another to restart it. Once she had been stabilised I was then sent home in a taxi and could only hope that my eight-year-old sister had not woken up to find that she was alone in the house.

My mother was the bravest woman I ever knew, and she fought like a tigress to stay with and raise her two daughters, but I have no memories of her as a well woman. My childhood experiences left me with a pathological fear of illness. I become almost rigid with fright when a loved one develops even the merest hint of a sniffle, assuming that it will, in fact, turn out to be viral pneumonia and lead to imminent death. I never visit the doctor for myself in case he should tell me something I don't want to hear, not that I fear death (I don't) but I am terrified of the mode of deliverance.

To add to all of this, Kenny's father died from gastric cancer at the age of twenty nine, and Kenny knew that my biggest fear was that he should meet the same fate, and for these reasons he had persuaded the specialist to change the diagnosis on the form knowing full well that I would take it from him at the first opportunity. His quiet strength is something that I still miss every single day.

Let battle commence

I have always been a scrapper in the sense that I am distinctly ill at ease with defeat. I used to view my tenacity as a strength, but sometimes my inability to recognise and accept the point at which the game is finally over can be my greatest weakness too. After the initial shock of the diagnosis, I launched a full-on assault against the tumour in my husband's stomach: if I could no longer deny that it existed, then I was bloody well determined that it was not going rob me of him or our future together. The stakes were as high as they get and defeat was NOT an option, so I began to rally the troops like never before.

First up, I read just about everything ever written about gastric cancer, devouring complex medical studies in the hope of discovering a new and innovative treatment, only to find that this type of cancer is relatively under-researched in comparison to other forms of the disease. Medically at least, Kenny's treatment plan was pretty much all there was. The only good news at this time was that the cancer had not spread and was still contained within the walls of the stomach. It was proposed that a course of chemotherapy would shrink the tumour to a size that would allow for its removal, along with Kenny's stomach, which we were told he would be able to live without. Further chemotherapy would mop up any remaining cancer cells with *curative intent*, a phrase I clung onto with all the same tenacity that a fat girl fighting eviction from the basket of a deflating hot air balloon full of anorexics might employ.

Eat to live

The internet, at this point in my life, was something of a mystery to me, though I quickly realised its value in researching a potential cure for my husband's cancer, which apparently was going to be nowhere as difficult as I might have imagined. I discovered a myriad of pills, potions and meditation therapies to name but a few, all claiming to be a cure, though, to anyone who hasn't actually got cancer or who isn't close to someone who has, these are all frankly laughable. Kenny himself remained as pragmatic as ever – even when I tried to persuade him that we could cure him with baking soda, he conceded that, yes, it may well have helped me with my frequent bouts of cystitis, and it was also good at raising my homemade bread but this did not necessarily mean that it would prove to be as effective at raising the dead.

My next attempt at achieving a miracle had slightly more gravitas to it, in that the evidence in favour of nutrition-based therapies appears to have more of a scientific bias to them. Certain foods when eaten in sufficiently large quantities, it was claimed, could achieve remission in some cancer patients. I managed to sell this one to Kenny on the basis that he needed to be as fit as possible in order to withstand the gruelling bouts of chemo that he was about to face. There were some not insignificant challenges in the application of this nutritional based approach. Kenny's requirements where food was concerned were simple enough, i.e. if it looked, tasted and acted like a bacon sandwich then he would be happy to eat it, but he considered all types of vegetables - with the exception of processed peas - to be alien life forms and, a salad was never going to find its way into his gastrointestinal tract as long as he remained in charge of his mouth.

The tumour affected his ability to swallow and, despite him telling me this often, I simply could not understand why he would refuse the soups, smoothies and juices into which I had blended all manner of cancer-fighting ingredients if there was even the slightest chance it might save his life. Frustrated with by what I saw as his lack of co-operation, I even accused him of wanting to leave me, assuring him in my ignorance that, had the boot been on the other foot, I would have happily consumed the produce of several large allotments if it meant staying with him. The look on his face in response was one I will have to live with for the rest of my life.

I was forced to acknowledge that if my husband was going to be cured of his cancer it was not going to be achieved by force-feeding him, so I stopped trying to do so, partly because by then I had stumbled across something I considered a much more serious contender for a cure.

Run from the cure

I came across the above-named documentary online about a Canadian guy called Rick Simpson, who says that he cured his own cancer by extracting a compound called THC (tetrahydrocannabinol) from marijuana, which he then made into an oil. He claims to have cured people from very advanced and end-stage cancers. Now living in Croatia after the Canadian authorities prosecuted him for his activities, his claims are backed up by both anecdotal and some scientific evidence.

It became quickly apparent that cannabis oil was not a product that was going to land on my doorstep courtesy of Amazon, so I decided to research the options at my disposal which included the possibility of manufacturing it myself. I came across some instructions on YouTube and, if I had found the whole *carrot gate* episode to be something of a challenge, the prospect of trying to produce cannabis oil in a domestic kitchen with only a video for guidance was to take the meaning of the word to a whole different level. As someone who was once caught out wiping away white powder from beneath her septum, but only as a result of an altercation with her sherbet fountain, the prospect of sourcing industrial strength weed in a sufficient quantity was a daunting prospect in itself.

The next problem involved an arguably higher level of risk. Assuming that I was successful in sourcing the raw materials that I needed to make the oil, the next step of the process required that they are then soaked in a high strength and very flammable solvent whilst applying gentle heat which, if not gentle enough, had the potential to leave my smouldering slippers behind, as the only remaining testament to my existence. Ensuring the correct ventilation would be crucial in order to prevent a build-up of explosive fumes, but as cannabis is not exactly the shrinking violet of the plant world when it comes to smell, I worried that its pungent and highly recognisable odour would then waft its way through the wide-open kitchen windows and attract the unwanted attention of our neighbours. As I imagined the presence of more twitching noses outside our house than you would reasonably expect to find at a Beatrix Potter convention, it felt as though the harder I tried to *run towards the cure*, the *cure*, had donned racing spikes and was speeding away in the opposite direction.

Obtaining the elusive oil occupied my thoughts almost constantly. Exhausted and frustrated I fell into bed at night beside my husband knowing that his options were narrowing by the hour and, with this preying heavily on my mind, I dreamt that despite all the legal and safety implications we finally had our miracle cure within our grasp. I was ecstatic and keen to administer the first dose of the oil as soon as possible and, after reading the instructions in this respect, gave Kenny some oil the size of a grain of rice which needed to be placed under the tongue and increased gradually in small increments.

The morning after Kenny had received his first dose, he seemed to have enjoyed a reasonably restful night and on waking, he requested that we go to McDonald's to get some ice-cream. I was quite shocked by this as Kenny, like me, was not a fan of fast food and he had certainly never shown much of a penchant for ice cream before either but, as a trip to McDonald's would involve calories and lots of them, I bundled him into the car before he had a chance to remember either of these things. I made a mental note to self to try and not to watch him eat each mouthful. Apart from annoying him intensely, Kenny said that I was also inclined towards the opening and closing of my mouth which made him feel like a baby in a high chair being encouraged to feed by its mother.

By the time he had consumed the third spoonful of strawberry ice-cream without complaint, I could barely contain my excitement when suddenly he put his spoon down and demanded to be taken home. I tried hard to hide my disappointment but cheerily suggested he might manage to eat more after his next dose of oil, but Kenny was adamant that he would not be back. He explained that whilst I thought he was resting he believed, he spent the previous night in McDonald's eating strawberry ice-cream from a bucket with a shovel, but began to suspect that something wasn't quite right when, during this visit, his ice-cream arrived in a small plastic pot served with a spatula and tasted like shit. Now my research into the use of cannabis oil had assured me that it did not produce any of the same hallucinogenic effects as smoking it did, a fact I was keen to point out to Kenny, who then queried the dosage. I referred him to the instructions and showed him where it said that the initial dose should be equivalent in size to that of a grain of rice, at which point he threw his arms in the air and informed me that only I could have thought that a chicken nugget was comparable in size to that of a grain of rice.

The morning proper arrived and I was devastated to learn that my vivid dream had been nothing more than a product of my frustration at being denied the chance to fully explore this chance of a cure for my husband. Whilst governmental attitudes towards the use of medicinal cannabis appear to be softening, if not exactly thawing, I am still angry that those who are desperate to trial a drug which, might have a potentially beneficial effect on a range of health conditions, still face being criminalised for doing so.

The first three months of chemotherapy seemed to have gone to plan. Kenny tolerated the treatments reasonably well, and both his appetite and energy levels improved sufficiently for us to even enjoy a short break in Cornwall. We were convinced that the improvements in his health had been brought about because the tumour was shrinking, and we began to prepare ourselves to face the surgery that would, once and for all, remove the cancer that had so cruelly turned our lives upside down.

There was no attempt made to soften the brutal verdict when it came, and this time there was no way that Kenny could have protected either me or himself from it. He was told in a manner devoid of any compassion whatsoever that, not only had the chemotherapy proved ineffective against the tumour but that it may have actually accelerated its growth, which meant that, as it was now invading the pancreas, surgery would no longer be possible. In that one brief moment, our all-important hope of treatment with *curative intent* was gone. By way of a consolation prize, Kenny was offered another round of chemotherapy which, if he was lucky, might extend his life by another six months, but ultimately his condition was now deemed incurable and terminal. Much like I did when I first learned of his diagnosis, my instinct was to run, but this time my legs were too leaden to move, whilst my husband's response was as succinct and to the point as ever when he described his situation as *a bit of a bummer*. After a two hour wait to get the revised prognosis, we were then ushered back out into the crowded waiting room, all in less than five minutes. My inability to stifle my violent sobs would have done very little to provide reassurance to those sat awaiting verdicts of their own, but I do remember being so angry at the time that in a perverse way I actually derived some pleasure from this.

Addenbrookes hospital – Cambridge

Kenny's response to his revised prognosis remained, at least outwardly, to be typically philosophical. Whilst he didn't want to die at the age of fifty-six and readily agreed to the second line chemotherapy treatment in the hope of more time, if not an actual cure, he was largely accepting of the fact that his survival was now beyond his control. I, on the other hand, was completely incapable of leaving my husband's longevity in the hands of fate and, even though logically I knew that our backs were up against the wall, I still refused to accept that my husband was going to die.

In early June 2014, Kenny started his next course of chemotherapy, which this time around was nothing short of vicious. It wiped out his immune system, exposing him to one infection after another, each of which was a threat to his life in themselves. He was no longer able to eat more than a few mouthfuls of chocolate mousse, and his skeleton became clearly visible beneath the virtually transparent covering of his skin. I knew that time was running out and we needed to do something radical and, we needed to do it sooner rather than later.

I was vaguely aware at the time that Wilco Johnson, the musician of Dr Feel Good fame, had been given a diagnosis of pancreatic cancer and that his prognosis was also terminal. However, it was now being reported in the press that Mr Johnson had been given a slim chance of survival, in the form of a radical new procedure to remove both his pancreas and his stomach. I tuned into every news bulletin I could after he underwent the surgery, willing him to survive because I thought that if he could, then so could my husband.

I contacted the same surgeon who had operated on Wilco Johnson at Addenbrooks hospital in Cambridge, and he agreed to take a look at Kenny's medical records. It was the most tenuous of lifelines but, after having reviewed the files, he contacted us to say they wanted to admit Kenny as soon as possible. I can only describe that moment as one of horrible excitement. The prospect that surgery might still be a possibility was undeniably exciting, but daring to hope was also a painful risk because we were rapidly running out of stones to look underneath and corners in which to shine a torch.

Kenny's condition continued to deteriorate evermore rapidly and, by the time we reached the hospital in Cambridge, he was at the stage where he didn't even have the strength to stop his head lolling onto his chest. As ridiculous at it sounds, I seriously considered sticking a wooden pole inside the back of his jumper, so that I could tape his head to it, to try and make him appear fit enough to withstand the surgery. The surgeon explained that Kenny's latest scans and X-rays all showed that the cancer was still contained within the walls of his stomach and though the tumour was pushing up against the pancreas, it was not as yet invading it. If an exploratory procedure confirmed that there were no other signs of cancer external to this then, yes, technically surgery was still possible, but would ultimately depend on an assessment of Kenny's fitness to survive such an invasive operation. To help build up his strength it was proposed that a feeding tube was fitted during the exploratory procedure to deliver some much-needed nutrition.

Having spent so much of my life around members of the medical profession, I am very adept at reading faces that try to conceal bad news and, when the nurse taking my husband back to the ward failed even once to meet my gaze in favour of vague chit chat, I knew the worst well before the surgeon was able to confirm it. What looked like tiny cancerous cells had been found on a gland leading to the liver and, whilst testing would be needed to confirm it absolutely, it looked as though the cancer had spread and, consequently, there was nothing else that could be done. The feeding tube had been fitted so that Kenny would at least no longer have to endure the agony of eating for himself, which was a small but significant improvement in what was left in both the quality and quantity of his life.

Time's up

My husband was discharged from Addenbrookes on the 10th July 2014 on what was his 57th birthday and, once he blew out the candles on a birthday cake he couldn't eat, I quickly resumed my quest for a cure, conceding only that it would now require a miracle, but that they did sometimes happen. Kenny was completely unable to sit up or lie down at this stage, and his legs filled with fluid which made them so heavy he could not walk unaided. I simply dressed them day and night and bought a foot massager recommended by the cricketer Ian Botham which claimed to reduce swelling in the ankles and feet. As his liver began to be affected and his stomach filled with ascites, I took him to the hospice to have a drain fitted which was so painful that even a cocktail of drugs that would have taken down a small horse, let alone a man of Kenny's dwindling stature, failed to have any effect, but none of this made any difference to my belief that I would somehow save my husband.

One evening, as we sat quietly together, Kenny looked up and gave me that dazzling smile of his, and for a split second the cheeky Irish chappie I loved with all my heart was back in the room. He asked me if I thought that the time had come for us to admit defeat and to finally throw in the towel. Horrified by what I was hearing, my response was an unequivocal no, and I continued to insist that we might still be able to find him a medical trial or another doctor. Despite my protestations, I know now, as I probably knew then, that Kenny had simply reached the limits of his capacity to fight for his survival and was asking for my permission to go on ahead alone, but I was simply unable to give it. He died the following night.

I have never been big on regret, though of course there have been times in my life when I have felt that I could or should have done things differently. With the benefit of hindsight, I realise that I might have focused more on Kenny himself, and what little time we had left together, and less on his illness and a fight against it that I quite literally took to his death. My husband was always something of a fatalist, though, and he firmly believed that things happen in the way that they do because we are each powerless to do them any differently, though this knowledge does not stop me wishing sometimes that I had.

Chapter 2

The beginning of the end

Widow brain

The first days and weeks after Kenny died are difficult to recall with any clarity. *Widow Brain* is a phenomenon which is scientifically recognised as a mechanism that protects a newly bereaved spouse from the shock and reality of their situation, and it is pretty effective in achieving this. In my case, the ability to finish a complete sentence disappeared overnight, I forgot how to drive, and the tiredness was so overwhelming that I was rarely awake for more than a few hours at a time. This can be a real handicap when it comes to dealing with the bureaucracy of death. My use of vodka in copious amounts at this time did little to help with my levels of consciousness but, strangely, did not seem to stop me from retaining a minimal degree of functionality, though I did wake up with a headache each morning and a tongue that stuck to the roof of my mouth with all the tenacity of a fuzzy felt sheep. The rest of the time I was content to spend in a state of oblivion because this was a state I fully intended to make more permanent, once I had *killed off* my husband in the official sense.

I didn't have a drink when I went to see Kenny in the chapel of rest, which is probably the only reason I can recall having been there at all, though I do remember that I was very excited by the prospect of seeing him again, even if he was dead. I rang the doorbell at the chapel of rest and was greeted by deep melancholy chimes that I half expected to be answered by Herman Munster. Even though I knew exactly where I was, and why I was there, I felt strangely detached from reality, almost as though I was an actress playing a role. Once my husband had been prepared for his visitor, I was taken into to a small recess in the chapel where he was resting and the sudden drop in temperature caused me to shiver, as heat is neither necessary nor desirable around the dead.

I stood for a while looking at my husband. The body in the coffin resembled the man I knew and loved but was now devoid of everything that he had been. I reached out and placed my hand onto his chest, which was unnaturally icy to the touch, but I was pleased to see that, despite the ravages of his illness, he looked very smart in his pinstripe suit and brand new gleaming white shirt. I knew that Kenny would have considered the shirt an altogether unnecessary expense given that the crematorium was his next and final destination. He was undeniably tighter than two coats of paint when it came to spending money on himself but generous to a fault with everyone else, so buying him a particularly expensive shirt because, for once, he was powerless to stop me was hugely satisfying at the time. My amusement, however, was not destined to last when I arrived at the till to pay for the shirt, and discovered that it had been reduced to half price in a flash sale. If Kenny had not actually been involved in the pulling of some celestial strings himself, he certainly would have appreciated the impromptu discount, which was enough to convince me that I should buy him a nice new pair of shoes to wear for his date at the crematorium too.

I told Kenny all the latest football results and about my plans for his funeral, trying to adjust to the fact that he would never again laugh with me, take the piss, or even shout at me, when I suddenly became utterly convinced that his chest had started to rise and fall. Startled by this, I briefly wondered if I should shout out to someone for help but, as I watched the sunlight streaming in through the stained glass windows of the chapel of rest, and confirmed that the brass plate on the lid of the coffin did indeed have my husband's name etched into it, I was forced to conclude that calling for the services of a paramedic at this juncture was unlikely to improve matters. I leaned over and gently kissed my husband on his cheek for the last time, before telling him that I loved him and that I would be following along very soon.

Religion

Kenny was brought up in the Catholic faith or, more accurately, would have been if his love of football had not meant more to him than the teachings of a faith he neither understood nor felt he needed in his life. Both of his brothers were altar boys who sang in the church choir and one evening their priest arrived at the family home to visit Kenny's mother, to extol upon her the various virtues of her two sons. The cleric was somewhat bemused, though, when she inquired as to the progress of her youngest son, Kenneth, as he had been totally ignorant of the fact that a third sibling even existed. So it came to pass that on the following Sunday morning Kenny was unceremoniously dragged off the football pitch by the priest, who then promptly installed him into a church pew instead, via a lengthy session in the confessional box.

I married Kenneth Dominic Manning when I was just eighteen years old, albeit an eighteen year old with big hair, an even bigger attitude and who was, by then, already running the first of many business ventures. I had been brought up by protestant church-going parents and, as a child, diligently attended Sunday school until one week I announced that I would no longer be doing so. I had decided that as my search for the *meaning of life* had proved fruitless within the confines of my own church, the time had come for me to look elsewhere for this elusive concept. Despite enjoying the gospel singing at the local Tabernacle and being moderately impressed by the doctrines of the Spiritualist church, who do at least try to evidence their belief in the afterlife, I remained pretty faithless. The *meaning of life* is not much clearer to me now than it was all those years ago, though I am no longer sure that it really matters in the grand scheme of things.

When they discovered that Kenny intended to marry someone outside of their religion this was, for his family, unthinkable. Whilst I understood and respected the role of religion in their lives, I was opinionated and unfettered by the fear of hell and damnation, all facets of my personality that made me an unlikely candidate for conversion to the Catholic faith. If religion had been important to my future husband and given my own ambivalence towards it, I might have felt differently but, just because I was the wrong religious flavour in the eyes of his family, was not enough of a reason for me to acquiesce to their demands. In the spirit of compromise, I did agree to a pre-wedding meeting with a priest who hoped that he would be able to convince me that converting to Catholicism was not only a desirable thing to do but a necessary one. Given that my previous flirtation with religion hadn't led to a spiritual awakening of any kind, I was less than hopeful that one might manifest after such a visit but decided that I would at least keep an open mind to the possibility.

On my arrival at the Rectory, I was shown to a seat in a dark imposing room lined from floor to ceiling with books. The titles on their spines were obscured by a thick layer of dust, which suggested that the contents of these colossal volumes were probably not your actual page-turners.

After the initial pleasantries were exchanged, I politely declined the priest's offer of a large balloon of brandy on the grounds that I suspected that this was a cynical ploy, aimed at helping him in his manipulations of what, he clearly hoped, would be a malleable teenager. The cleric began the first of his lengthy monologues but I was soon distracted by his tendency to punctuate them with a twisted grin that revealed a collection of rotten stumps hidden behind it when he did. Occasionally, saliva would spill onto his chin, which he wiped away with a handkerchief the colour of coal.

Held as I was in a kind of grotesque thrall, I had to ask him to repeat his contention that the sovereign state of the Vatican City was an institution of untold wealth, failing to see the spiritual significance of his statement. Reaching inside his cassock the priest rummaged around under it in the area of his groin, panting heavily from the effort, when to my eventual relief, he proudly produced a twenty-pound note a significant amount of money in the 1970s. He placed the note on a velvet lined salver, which contained at least six others of the same denomination. The money, he explained, had been given to him by members of his congregation to offer up prayers on their behalf. When I asked what happened to the donations, it was said that they helped to ensure that the Catholic Church remained financially independent and, therefore, answerable only to God. Confused by this answer, I queried the plight of the starving, homeless and all those displaced by wars, often caused by differences in religion. Even I would have struggled to get a word in with God at twenty quid a time, so how on earth would people like these be able to afford it? This question was followed by a sip taken from the brandy balloon, as my unfiltered eighteen-year-old mouth went on to espouse a somewhat simplistic solution. I suggested that it might help to ensure a fairer system of wealth distribution if the church sold some of the treasures stored in the Vatican. This money could then be used to help all the aforementioned disadvantaged groups who, after all, were perfectly capable of praying for themselves for free. I stopped when I realised I that my suggestion of flogging off the family silver, and essentially cutting out the middle man, had, judging by the size of the cleric's next gulp of brandy, seemed to have gone down about as well as a rogue fart might in a library. This marked the starting point in a definite downward spiral.

The conversation continued without reference to my thoughts concerning the fiscal arrangements of the church and was suddenly propelled into a very different direction.

Talking now about the teachings of the church in respect of contraception and, careful to make no mention of actual sex, I was told in the kind of tone used in a book aimed at five year old's that the Catholic faith allowed only the rhythm and natural methods of preventing the conception of a child. All children, it was explained, were acts of God and it was sinful to use artificial methods to obstruct the will of the divine. Following the priest's own example of not using any type of language that might imply that sex was now the topic of discussion, I used a simple analogy of my own. I asked who it was that would take care of all the little acts of God that were created every time their parents decided to park their cars in a nice warm garage, instead of leaving it outside on the forecourt as the church decreed they should. The cleric once again retreated into the sanctity of his glass and, through gritted teeth, or what was left of them, would only say we were all the children of God and, that it was He Himself who would provide. In light of our previous conversation concerning the starving and homeless, this seemed to me to suggest that God had not read His job description properly. So far, my suspicions were all but confirmed that this was a religion which relied heavily on control and, in this respect, there was to be one more element to the priest's Holy Trinity.

Catholicism, I was solemnly advised, was a lifelong commitment. The church saw it as their absolute duty to support the odd lapse, but ex-communication was a serious last resort, which could be visited on whole families and not just the miscreant. I doubted that ex-communication was applicable in this particular instance, but I suspected that my refusal to be gathered in, was the real reason behind the priest's suggestion that my actions, could lead to the expulsion of Kenny's whole family from the flock too. I was told that if this were to happen my husband would inevitably come to resent me and, would then experience an irresistible urge to return to the bosom of the church. I think my brief silence, as I pondered my response, was interpreted by the priest as a sign of a weakening stance but was, in fact, because the meeting was drawing towards the outer limits of its usefulness in my eyes.

I politely thanked my host and told him that I agreed with him that it was highly likely that Kenny *would* experience an urge but it was far more likely to involve *my* ample bosom than that of the church. It was also quite usual during the process of satisfying this particular urge for Kenny to leave his car parked inside my nice warm garage because, thanks to some little pink pills I was taking, it was no longer necessary to whip it back out onto the forecourt when it sprang a leak. I threw a fiver onto the salver told the priest to pray for a clean handkerchief, a set of new dentures and a feather duster for his housekeeper.

Kenny and I were married on the 1st July 1978 at All Saints Stand, a venue selected for no other reason than it would look good on the photographs and, with the exception of the weddings of others, the inevitable round of Christenings, funerals and hostelries with the word Church in their name, religion played no further part in our lives together and nor would it at his funeral.

The Funeral

I regarded Kenny's funeral to be the very last thing that I could do for him and I wanted it to be a celebration of the man he was and of the life that we had shared together. When this was done it was very much my intention to tie up any loose ends and join my husband. This was not because I expected that we would meet at Heaven's gate and get to pick out a cloud together or, for that matter, a shared cell in the bowels below if our karmic bank did not have enough credit in its coffers for upstairs, but because I truly felt that going on without Kenny was pointless and, to me, oblivion was far preferable to pointless.

Somehow the appropriate arrangements were made, largely by good luck than good judgement, and the day of the funeral arrived. Mourners began to arrive in the form of friends and family, both old and new, and these emotional reunions threatened to overwhelm me so, whilst I had not intended to drink before the funeral, I found myself resorting to a familiar coping mechanism. The desired effect was quickly achieved and, as I began to relax, I convinced myself that another drink might serve to make the tribute I had written, to read at the funeral, a bit more entertaining as a result. I managed to down another two light beers before the hearse containing the body of my husband arrived at the front door.

The chapel of rest, where Kenny had lain ahead of his funeral, was only a short distance from the crematorium which was to be his final destination, but I had specifically wanted him to start his last journey from the home we had built together. This meant that we needed to travel much further as a consequence and the logistics of which deserved much greater consideration than the scant regard I had given them.

When it came time to leave, I took a moment to look at the floral tributes in the hearse surrounding Kenny's coffin, briefly thinking that at least the beautiful floristry surrounding him couldn't trigger his hay fever on this occasion. The undertaker gave me a small velvet pouch containing my husband's wedding ring and asked for my door key so he could lock the house, but just as the cortege began to move slowly away I spotted my cousin banging frantically on the front window. A last-minute, unavoidable call of nature had meant that the house had turned into the equivalent of the Marie Celeste on his return from answering it. This incident caused much laughter and I thought how very appropriate it was that, for a man who loved to laugh at life as much as Kenny did, his funeral proceedings had started with the sound of lots of it.

My two young grandsons travelled with me and their father in the car directly following the hearse. The bond between the boys and their granddad had been a very close and special one but, at the ages of four and six years old, they were not yet capable of comprehending the permanence of death. Kayden, the youngest of the boys, asked me if his granddad was inside that funny shaped box in the car in front and I replied that he was. He thought about this for a moment before asking if his Granddad had known everything. I, of course, couldn't resist replying that nobody knew *everything,* but it was quite possible that his Granddad thought that *he* did, this, despite being a self-confessed Manchester United fan. My attempt at humour was lost on my grandson who said simply that, if his Granddad really did know everything, he would have got himself out of that silly box so that he could sit on his knee like always. I never knew until then that even silent tears make a noise.

It is a fact that middle-aged ladies are often the owners of bladders that shrink to the size of a walnut over time; add to this a large vodka, two beers and a funeral procession travelling at twenty miles per hour, with the effect of extending a twenty-minute journey by a further forty, then a state of emergency is very likely to exist. After a torturous last three miles, the gates of the crematorium finally came into view and relief was within reach. The cortege drew to a standstill at the front of the chapel, at which point car doors were flung open in urgent unison. The apologetic nature of bow legged and bent over mourners racing each other at speed in order to achieve pole position for the toilets, was reminiscent of something from a Benny Hill sketch, as the air of funereal farce continued.

I followed Kenny's coffin into the chapel to the strains of '*Jesu Joy of Mans Desiring*', a hymn that had been sung at our wedding and which he had specifically requested, though I was surprised that he had remembered it. I watched my sister take her place with the other male pallbearers with a mixture of pride and sorrow as she carried the man she credited as having carried her many times throughout her life, as she now did for him in death. Soon it would be my turn to pay my own tribute delivered, as it would be, with a heavy heart but, thankfully by now, an empty bladder.

Goodbye sweetheart

'Well, my darling, you always said that I had to have the last word and, as usual, you are right, though I wish with all my heart that you would interrupt me again in that annoying way you always did when I tried to express it. Our amazing adventure began when we were just kids. You liked Boddingtons beer, Manchester United and your Benny Goodman trousers which, contained enough material to make tents in sufficient numbers for several large refugee camps. But, of course, you liked me too and it wasn't long before I fell for your cheeky chappie charm

After we were married, we spent about three quid on a honeymoon in Blackpool, as it was pretty much all we had to our name. Unable to afford to buy more than one drink in a nightclub, you were thrilled when a bottle of champagne arrived at our table, courtesy of a stranger sitting at a table in the corner. At least you were up until the point he tried to kiss you on the way to the toilet, after which we made a quick exit and went and drank orange juice in our room.

In the early days, when money was tight, we used to upend the furniture, searching for any spare change lurking there, so that we could buy something to eat. One time we found enough to buy a packet of Wonder Mash and a tin of baked beans, only to discover that the Wonder Mash was full of onion pieces, which you absolutely hated, so I ate the mash whilst you ate the beans, and then shared the after-effects with me for the rest of the evening, claiming that, as we had no money for heating either, I should be grateful for the regular blasts of warm air.

We worked hard together in our various businesses. One day a six-foot gentleman helped himself to a large bottle of sherry and walked out of our off-licence without paying for it. You, my darling, were nowhere near six foot in height but, with your Irish dander up and a baseball bat in your hand you were more than capable of causing the type of involuntary reaction that usually necessitates a change of underwear. You managed to get your man, along with a reprimand from the police, who told you that, as a result of meeting you, the poor thief had been considerably traumatized. It was later discovered that he was responsible for a spate of burglaries in the area, after which you became something of a local hero. Kenny, you always have been, and always will be a hero to me, though, perhaps, with the exception of the time you visited the tip and returned with a wooden commode that you then proudly presented to my poor disabled mother who, for reasons you could never fully understand, was not completely delighted with her gift.

You will be pleased to learn that I am now out of therapy after being forced to watch your limbo at a Hawaiian night in Florida and I have finally forgiven you for the oven glove you bought me from a bargain store. I suppose you weren't to know it was made from tissue paper and the plastic surgery means that you can hardly see the scars at all now.

I am so happy that we were able to take our lovely grandsons, Kian and Kayden, to Captiva Island, our special place. You taught them to fish on the Gulf of Mexico and never complained once when their wuss of a father refused to unhook his catfish without your help, all whilst screaming like a girl when you did. You simply explained to them that this type of behaviour was quite common amongst Manchester City supporters and we all laughed uncontrollably at your antics on the T dock during what was to be your last holiday on Captiva. I cannot express how much I miss the sound of your laughter already.

It is my deepest regret that I could not find a way of standing firm between you and the door marked exit. My strength was you: you knew how to fuel my successes, always able to say the most inappropriate things at exactly the right times, whilst holding on to my ankles when my feet threatened to leave the floor. We were, and are, a team and this divide called death will prove to be no barrier to the love that we shared unconditionally with each other for the greater part of each of our lifetimes. Goodbye for now, sweetheart – we had the most amazing adventure and, for that, I thank you from the bottom of my heart'.

When the service came to an end and it was time to leave my husband for the final time, I approached his coffin and placed a small light bulb on the top of it. I had insisted that the doors be left open during the committal and, in doing so, robbed the Catholic contingent of the last vestige of anything vaguely familiar to them, something I considered small payback for having deprived a young boy of his dreams of becoming a footballer during his Sunday mornings in the park. The sound of the Manchester band James singing '*Moving On*' was not enough to drown out Kayden's hysterical screams when it finally dawned on him that his granddad was going to stay in that funny shaped box and was bound for a place we could not travel to with him. At least, not yet.

Chapter 3

All our yesterdays

A cunning plan

Given that I wasn't expecting to need it for much longer, I continued with the systematic abuse of my liver and began to put my affairs in order, hoping to minimise any disruption caused by my demise. It was only a few short weeks after the funeral and already most of the well-meaning offers of support had disappeared more quickly than a Florida snowman, with the exception of my close family who did all they possibly could, but who ultimately had their own lives to lead.

In my more lucid moments, during the tying up of all those proverbial loose ends, I managed to stockpile enough packets of paracetamol to ensure an efficient and speedy departure. One evening I had reached the point at which, now, seemed as good a time as any to execute my plan. My evenings, since Kenny died, were usually spent with a glass of vodka in one hand and my laptop in the other. If my dependence on alcohol during this period was fairly self-explanatory, then the amount of time I spent browsing the internet was perhaps less so. Before Kenny became ill it would be fair to describe my IT skills as on a par with those of a cardboard box but, during the months of his illness when I was searching desperately for a cure, I developed a modest degree of proficiency though, still considered the likes of social media sites to be the exclusive domain of the brain dead. During Kenny's illness, I joined an online forum for those suffering from gastric cancer, in the hope that I might find something that would help my husband but, instead, all the familiar names began to disappear one by one, only to later reappear in a group for widows and widowers instead. This was one promotion I was determined to resist. I went and gathered my secret stash of paracetamol from their various hiding places and liberated around a hundred tablets from the confines of their blister packs, before pouring myself another two large vodkas, one to enjoy and one to wash down all the pills lying next to me.

My original plan of despatch was that I would drive up the long quarry road a short distance from my house, where I would take the tablets under the cover of darkness and, in an attempt at protecting my own family from making the grim discovery of my remains, I had magnanimously elected to inflict this particular honour on the quarry workers turning up for their shift the following morning instead. The only problem with this particular plan was that, because of the amount I was drinking, I wasn't capable of even seeing my car, let alone navigating it along a dark country road with a seventy miles per hour speed limit. I decided that, because I had absolutely no desire to hurt anyone other than myself, my suicide would need to take place in my own home after all. I left instructions for whoever it was that arrived on the scene not to enter the room where I was, but to call for the emergency services instead, before sticking the directive on the door.

For reasons I will never fully understand, or indeed need to, whilst enjoying what I fully expected to be the penultimate alcoholic drink of my life, I elected to log on to the widow's group online. As I waited for my laptop to boot up, I contemplated the pile of white pellets beside me and I remember thinking how incredibly easy it was to invite death when you desired it, and yet it was a state so very difficult to repel when you did not. I took about six of the tablets, wondering how it would feel to die: would I know when it was actually happening, would there be any tunnels of light involved, or floating above my own body as I zipped along the celestial highway? I concluded that I would know the answers to all of these questions soon enough, so I momentarily turned my attentions back to my laptop even though, by now, I could hardly figure out what the words swimming by on the screen in front of me were saying.

My ability to type had been reduced to random stabbing movements roughly aimed at the keyboard but, somehow, I did manage to write something and pressed send. I didn't expect or need a response which, to be honest, could only have come from a Spanish speaking Scandinavian who also had a tenuous grasp of Mandarin thrown in. I returned to my pile of paracetamol to finally learn if I was destined to hail a heavenly taxi, or was heading into eternal darkness. I don't remember when everything went black but, as I became aware of light beginning to permeate my barely open eyelids, my surroundings confirmed that the taxi had been an apparent no show – though the presence of a foul stench did lead me to wonder if I had been more successful in thumbing a lift to Hades.

Gradually I realised that the distinctly unholy smell was that of my own faeces. The skin on my face felt tight and I seemed to have developed strange lumps all over it, some of which fell off when I touched them. Instinctively I reached for my glass and was relieved to see a reasonable amount of vodka still left in it and, just as I was about to take a slug from it, I caught a glimpse of something in the large living room mirror in front of me. At least, now I had a diagnosis for the appearance of the strange detachable lumps on my face, which, it turned out, were paracetamol tablets that had become partially glued to my face by my own saliva. Having feared the sudden onset of leprosy, this was something of a result.

My heart was racing and the pounding in my head caused me to retch uncontrollably but, as I hadn't eaten for days, I was only able to produce thick yellow bile. If I was revolted and disgusted by the images unfolding before me in the mirror, then those feelings were as nothing compared to when I finally realised that my husband was a pile of dust and ashes residing in an undertaker's urn, a smiley face on a photograph and a series of memories destined to fade. I tried to scream but the empty air around me remained quite undisturbed by sound, so I crawled around on the floor pleading with Kenny to help me. I can't remember how long I remained in the eye of the storm but I was very aware that my sanity was at stake until, completely exhausted, I passed out again. When I came round for the second time I knew that, whilst there would likely be paler versions of it yet to come, there was no doubt in my mind that what I had just experienced had been my darkest hour.

Connections and Widow World

Following the failure of my cunning plan, I continued to spend my evenings drinking enough alcohol that, should the consumption of it ever be turned into an Olympic sport, I would have been guaranteed a place on the winner's podium. I did, however, flush my supply of paracetamol down the toilet, as I deduced that alcohol, without the aid of pills, would probably do the same job, even if it did take a bit longer. One evening I returned to the widow's site online to see what I had posted before passing out in my botched bid to leave the world which, until now, I had been far too embarrassed to re-visit.

'Knock, knock, you lot… guess what? I don't want to fucking come in – you can all piss off.'

I have translated this from the original text and tidied it up as best I can, but there was no one more surprised than me when I realised that my post actually had a response.

'Welcome to the group that no one wants to join.' I have never been a fan of stating the *bleeding obvious* and this was a phrase that I later came to hate with a passion.

'It is perfectly understandable that you don't want to take that forward step to enter here but, my friend, you may as well, because the floor behind you has already collapsed and going forward is the only choice you have.'

There could be no doubt that this was, in fact, a fair point very well made and, in the absence of any logical argument against it, I tentatively began to open up the lines of communication on Widow World, as I had started to affectionately refer to it. My membership credentials might have been cast iron, but I still didn't feel as though I belonged to this particular collective. Whilst I was posting on Widow World and making new connections as a result of this, I began to re-think my attitude to social media. Having previously regarded it as something used by sad lonely people without lives of their own, I was forced to admit that, if indeed this was the case, then I was more than adequately qualified to join this group too.

When I wasn't posting on Widow World or getting to grips with the *like* button on social media sites I spent many hours just browsing the internet finding stuff, which helped me to self-diagnose a whole raft of life-threatening illnesses, which I was subsequently able to cure on YouTube. The discovery of online shopping was nothing short of a revelation. This meant that I could now guarantee that a steady flow of Smirnoff was regularly delivered directly to my front door, which was particularly useful as walking in a straight line often proved to be something of a challenge.

In an effort to address concerns about my unhealthy habits at this time, I made some adjustments to my online shopping list to reflect this. By adding Orange juice to my vodka, this act alone meant that I had addressed at least one of my five a day and, as vodka is distilled from corn, at a stretch I could count that as another. I probably didn't cover myself in glory, though, when on one morning I invited a very pretty, and very young, delivery man from Asda to join me inside for a 10.00 am cocktail. A man running over hot coals with bare feet smeared in petroleum jelly could not have made a swifter exit – undeterred, I simply switched my allegiances to Tesco.

Another health concern at this time was muscle wastage, an unfortunate by-product of spending large amounts of time sitting at a laptop, immersed in a virtual world. Add to this the effects of a lack of sunlight on my vitamin D levels, and floppy limbs become something of an inevitability. There are not many Eureka moments in the dark early days of widowhood, but the moment I discovered that I could use my mobile phone to receive e-mails whilst away from my laptop was definitely up there with that moment when you learn that you can produce a fairly decent orgasm on your own. The fact that the only e-mails I was getting back then were usually from *Simply Be* telling me that they did dresses in my size of tent was of little consequence to me, I was *connected* and that was what really mattered.

I also convinced myself that there were actual benefits to consuming alcohol in the volumes I was at this time. By calculating that my calorific intake was sufficiently high without the interference of food, my decision to give up cooking, as an unnecessary use of my time, seemed to have been completely justified. On the downside, however, was the battery of packages that used to arrive on my doorstep courtesy of Amazon on most days of the week. Whilst none of the items that I ordered in the wee small hours, were ever useful or necessary, I knew that I had reached a particularly low point when, with no memory of having ordered it, I took delivery of a life-sized blue Smurf.

Posting on Widow World

The following is a post I wrote on Widow World concerning the condition of *cash incontinence*, a term I used to describe my period of profligate spending, which was by no means helped by equally excessive drinking. I wrote the following post about eleven weeks after Kenny died, and it's an example of how I was already using humour to talk about my experiences, which seemed to resonate with others.

Cash incontinence

'Ooookay people...I think I have been doing reasonably well nearly 11 weeks in. I have coped so far with the desolation, despair, tears, brain fog and fear etc. etc. But a worrying new symptom has emerged which needs nipping in the wallet straight away before I am forced to find a cardboard box and bag a place under the arches, with only a small bottle of Lambrusco held in hands covered in fingerless gloves for company.

My darling husband used to laugh at me because I always used to find it difficult to spend money on myself. Well, that changed! Now I can't seem to stop and, if he had lived through the shock of seeing this for himself, I'm sure even he would have questioned my purchase of a black and diamante toilet brush with matching soap dish and tea light holders. I mean why? In addition to these inexplicable purchases I have also bought two dresses in the last few days and all I can say about them is that a well-decorated Christmas tree would provide the perfect camouflage should I choose to stand next to it. I won't even mention the shoes, the colour of which could easily be picked up by the radar of a low flying aircraft, and the reaction from children and small dogs is such that it is a good job I have a soft spot for both. An idea will pop into my head and off to the shops I go to buy something else I neither want, need or like, though actually, I did quite like the silk sheets I bought last week, at least I did until I slid out of bed. This spending simply has to stop. I know I am probably trying to fill the hole left by my darling Kenny but, if I don't regain control soon, the hole will simply remain as deep as ever, but will also have a 'welcome to your new home' sign standing beside it. I intend to enrol with the CIA that's, Cash Incontinents Anonymous to the uninitiated. My name is Sandra and I spend money – there I have said it. Hope this works!'

The responses to my posts were invaluable in that they gave me a reason to want to get up each day to read them, and I began to understand that what I was going through was no more painful than the experiences of other contributors on Widow World, as I had arrogantly assumed that it was.

The following post is another example of the way in which I tried to discuss issues relevant to our group by using humour. Looking back now this was probably the conceptual stage of what was to become GOWNS, though I simply wrote from my heart and talked about all the things that bereaved spouses find themselves having to negotiate alone for the first time. I had no idea back then that even those outrageously sparkly dresses I had purchased, and subsequently consigned to the back of the wardrobe, would themselves become significant later on.

The day I told the kids the truth about B&Q

'Ooookay people...the buffet is all done, cakes are baked, truthfully? Well, I did bake cookies but bought the cakes from Asda to save time. I had a lovely chat with someone last night and was feeling quite chipper this morning, glad to see the sun and thinking that the

children (grandchildren) would be able to play out this afternoon. Pottering about in the kitchen I watched our neighbours surveying the damaged fences. I live in quite an exposed rural area and this is the time of year where everyone congregates to plan repairs. Bang! As I watched it hit me that Kenny would/should have been out there with his morning coffee putting the world, as well as the fences to rights as he has done at this time of year for as many years as I can remember, only he wasn't. It suddenly dawned on me that going out into the garden today may not prove to be as straightforward as I had thought, so I decided on direct action which meant a trip to B&Q for some fence paint, picking up my grandsons up on the way.

I am a little ashamed to admit this but, when the boys were smaller and Kenny and I wanted to get around the store with the minimum of fuss, we used to pretend that B&Q was 'Bob the Builders' theme park. The highlight of which was an ice-cream from the van always parked outside on a decent day. As I watched the two little chaps tuck into their cones this morning I felt the need to level with them. Bob didn't and never had lived at B&Q I explained, but before long both lads were laughing helplessly. Kian told me that I was 'well weird', actually this is quite a compliment in today's vernacular so I was quite chuffed that my street cred stock had increased so significantly. Then Kayden added that their granddad had told them both ages ago that Bob the Builder didn't live at B&Q, but had also said, that I would be upset if I ever found out, so the boys had continued the pretence for my sake.

I told someone last night that Kenny is still the cause of much laughter in our house and so it goes on. The next time the neighbours join forces, I am going to join them with my paint and help them mend and repair those fences as Kenny would have done, knowing that it isn't just panels of wood that he and I are still fixing together...but more...so very much more.

Hope everyone has a reason to smile too today'.

Some responses to my cash incontinence and Bob the builder posts – which have been anonymised for obvious reasons.

'Dear Sandra

You do have a wonderful way with a story. I hope I can eventually get it all together as you have.

'Hi Sandra

You actually made me laugh with your Bob the Builder story, something I haven't done in a long time. So thanks for that.

'Hi Sandra

Oh my goodness, have to admit I actually laughed out loud at your post, to the point my daughter was asking me why and now she is too.

Thanks for helping us to smile today. Lots of love.'

This next reply is from Jayne Benge, who was later to become not only my very good friend but a fellow collaborator in the GOWNS project.

'Hi Sandra

I'm stuck in a place I should be sharing with Steve. Easter has been so much harder than I ever thought. I guess for those of us who were working couples, Easter was a time to chill out and look forward to long summer nights. I've done nothing but paint decking spindles for the past 4 hours. Once I had finished it was 'that time', when we would have sat and admired our days' work and chilled with a few drinks and I feel very alone at the moment. Thanks for your story it always helps to smile. In my family, B&Q was a punishment my kids hated the place so if they were playing up, no naughty step in my house, just a very long walk up and down all the aisles at B&Q which me and Steve (aka Mr DIY) loved'.

Jayne wrote the above in 2015, having lost her beloved Steve in October 2014, some weeks after I lost Kenny in August of the same year. This was not the first of our communications but was certainly amongst the earlier ones.

The next post I include because it is a record of the progress I was clearly making, though again I did not recognise this as such at the time. I wrote it in June 2015, a couple of months before the first anniversary of Kenny's death. Whilst most people will recognise the emotional implications of losing a spouse, it is perhaps less obvious to see how the simple day to day tasks which we inherit can so easily cause confusion and despair.

Weeds & Lightbulbs

'Ooookay people... I think I am doing alright, by that I mean I still have days when I cry enough to cause a drought in my tear ducts but, by and large bit by bit, I am reaching a place of better focus, a place from which I can now take a glimpse of the future, and what I need to do to get there. All good right? Well, it would be if it wasn't for the blinking' weeds in my garden. I mean I had heard about dandelions but well, when Kenny was alive I never actually saw one. He wasn't exactly Percy Thrower, but his horticultural ability was sufficient to make our environment relatively weed-free. Of course, the rubbish weather has meant that not much has happened in the garden recently, at least until now. What the heck happens when the sun comes out? Who knew that weeds live in walls, under paths and must have been waiting for Kenny to depart, before emerging triumphant, laughing in the face of my ineptitude? Looking on the bright side we learned that my grandchildren have remembered what to do if they ever get lost, which is stay put and shout like mad, we would never have found them in the long grass otherwise.

Light bulbs need changing was another discovery I have made since August last year, along with the fact that my car was not frost-free in the winter as I had always believed, it seems that Kenny was a lot busier than he looked. I was quite pleased initially when I worked out which voltage bulb went where, and I have happily responded to the little flashes and tripped *electrics which indicate a change of bulb is necessary, but now I think the weeds and the bulbs have conspired against me. The weeds seem to like the chemicals I spray on them, I think they even expect nibbles and the bulbs are pinging for fun. So I have hired a gardener who looks like Arnie 'I'll be back' Schwarzenegger, and he will be here this afternoon at the same time as an electrician, who is going to replace all the bulbs in the house with mega lasting ones of daylight quality.*

It feels good to be taking back control, by tonight I'll be able to venture outside again and, when I come back in, I will no longer be in the dark- result! Today I have found a way to beat the knotweed and will emerge from a darker place into a lighter one, I'll take this every time. Next up is sorting out Kenny's shed, he once told me that bad things happened to people who went in there who weren't him, I'll keep you all posted. I hope good things happen for you all today however small and insignificant they might seem at the time they all add up'.

Some responses to my weeds and lightbulbs post.

'Hi Sandra

Changing lightbulbs- that's nothing! I was changing fuses this week!! I even tested the fuse from a lamp that was not working in another lamp. The fuse is not the problem – the lamp is kaput'.

'Hi Sandra

All these new jobs we are taking on! Each one achieved is a small victory, or that's how I see it. For me this week's achievements (or was it last week? Days roll into one) have been changing a bulb in the brake light of the car, the car manual was actually quite good.

The other one was the hedge. It needed cutting. Rather than get someone in, muppet here decided to buy a hedge trimmer and tackle the job myself. The hedge now looks like two dogs have chewed chunks out of the side and the top has a definite wave to it.

When you've finished with Arnie Sandra, maybe you could send him over - I could do with some help with the heavier jobs that's for sure!!

'Oh, Sandra,

You do make me chuckle. But I know what you mean. The first thing I had to master was recycling. I remember the week after my husband died standing on the drive looking at the boxes and weeping because I had not got a clue which box the old batteries, paper, plastic and million other things that we recycle went into. Thankfully, I have now got a first-class degree in recycling. Other things that I have mastered recently are the lawnmower and feeding the tortoises when they came out of hibernation. I am still in the very early days of strimmer control. Cooking is still something I am having to re-learn as the kitchen was my husband's domain. I can open a tin though'.

'Well done Sandra,

And everyone else who is learning how to take on new tasks. What a resourceful bunch we are even under the most difficult of circumstances. For me, it's culinary tasks which act as my Everest to conquer. My husband was the chef in our house, and I have had to learn that there are other useful appliances in a kitchen other than a kettle and a microwave!'

'Dear Sandra,

Great post which had me laughing in places and so pleased your grandsons were rescued. I hope you have returned from the shed in one piece. Thank you for showing us what we are capable of achieving'.

Widow World helped all of us so much back in those early days: lots of connections were made and alliances formed, though I could never have imagined how important some of those would prove to be. All I did know was that I was beginning to create an existence for myself that seemed to suggest that my life, though not as I would have wanted it, was still worth living and subsequently I had no further need of a plan, cunning or otherwise.

Chapter 4

A step forward in ill-fitting shoes

A Widow World Weekend

The responses to my posts online began to grow in number and I started to think about how the connections I was making might work outside of the virtual reality in which we had so far co-existed. So I plucked up enough courage to book myself onto a Widow World weekend to find out. Signing up for this was a massive step. Being a widow is not what defines me and I was very apprehensive about joining a group whose marital status was possibly the only thing that we had in common and, also, because this was the first time I had socialised outside of my usual circle since Kenny died. Digging deep, I pulled on my big girl pants, not that I own any other size, applied the age-old adage of *'nothing ventured, nothing gained'* and set off for Yorkshire with an open mind and an unpredictably squeaky bottom.

There were two ladies in particular that I wanted to meet on the basis of our online chats and telephone conversations and, as I negotiated checking into a hotel alone for the first time, I knew in an instant that the tall, striking and confident lady dragging a large box into the hotel reception was one of them. Denise and I hugged each other on sight we had shared far too much to regard each other as strangers even if we hadn't met in person until then. I gave her a hand to haul the large box up several steps which, she went on to explain, was a portable fridge. Denise did not like her Prosecco anything less than ice cold and, by travelling with her own means of keeping it that way, she greatly reduced her chances of ever having to drink an unacceptably warm aperitif. I suffer from full-blown insomnia so the fridge was installed in my room because the sound of the coolants motor running during the night would not disturb someone who would be awake for most of it anyway. Denise was, and is, a force of nature: her straightforward *can do* no-nonsense attitude was something I warmed to immediately.

Later, when we headed into the town centre to meet up with Jayne and the other members of the group, I immediately recognised the same discomfort in her demeanour that I could only hope that I had been more successfully able to disguise about my own. Meeting a group of strangers in a busy town centre on Saturday afternoon, whose only link is dead people, is frankly enough to scare anyone, but Jayne looked literally terrified.

A flurry of handshakes accompanied the usual pleasantries as introductions were made and, even during these early exchanges, it was clear that a very distinct hierarchy existed within the group, which seemed to be based on how many of the previous events you had attended. The higher this number then the higher your widow ranking was and, without anything in the way of consultation with those of us occupying the lower echelons of this stratum, the consensus of the group was that we should all set off in search of a cup of coffee.

As a child, I had once unwittingly downed a bottle of milk from a playground crate that had been left out in the full glare of the sun in the days of free school milk, and I never drank the stuff again or, indeed, any other drink which contained it. My own personal preference would have been for something a lot stronger than coffee, but then I did have something of a predilection for alcohol at this time.

The group set off en masse and I felt very much like a middle-aged schoolgirl, finding it necessary on occasion to break out into a little skip in order to keep sight of the teacher in front. In my youth, I had been a half-decent netball player and enjoyed team sports, so was not unfamiliar with the concept of exercise but, more latterly, I considered a short walk to the pub, where I would weight lift several drinks before walking back home again, to be more than a sufficient amount of it. If I was now having some cause to regret my blasé attitude towards my levels of personal fitness, then I was deeply regretting my choice of footwear. Whilst everyone else seemed to have had the foresight to encase their phalanges in shoes made by either North Face or Regatta, my own choice was more, shall we say, Jimmy Choo?

Both Denise and Jayne were neither encumbered by unsuitable shoes nor were they suffering from the effects of long hours sat on their arses at a laptop, slugging vodka. I could only groan inwardly as we passed not only several warm and welcoming hostelries but what looked, to me, to be perfectly acceptable coffee houses too. I was seriously beginning to wish that I had stayed in the hotel to babysit Denise's fridge when an establishment which offered all the required combinations of frothy mocha was agreed upon on at last.

Grateful for the respite, and glugging from a bottle of water like a newly rescued castaway, my choice of beverage was questioned by one of the senior members of the group who, on learning that I was drinking water because I didn't like coffee, suggested that had I made this known earlier, then we could have gone to the pub instead. My response was a smile of the type to at least equal Jack Nicholson's excellent effort in the film *'The Shining'.*

A small rebellion

The respite from the route march around the spa town of Harrogate was all too brief and the members of Widow World were soon back on their many feet, like a giant centipede on a mission. Unfortunately, by now, my own feet had swollen to something resembling the size of two sumo sized beetroot and would have been inclined to spill from even the generous confines of the type of shoe commonly worn by patients in a heart failure clinic, let alone an elegant stiletto. Hardly fit to hobble, never mind run, behind a group of determined widows and widowers, all equipped with stopwatches and sweatbands, I summoned up all my resolve and pressed on regardless.

During the effort of keeping up with those some twenty years my senior and trying, at the same time, not to sound as though I was breathing with the aid of a ventilator borrowed from Darth Vader, I was further impeded when the rivers of sweat so far held to account by my fringe, finally burst their banks. This had the effect of liquefying my thick black eyeliner on contact, taking with it any last vestiges of hope that my distress might have gone unnoticed. A fat middle-aged woman with eyes like a panda hobbling along behind a group of sprightly widows, wearing crystal-encrusted shoes worthy of an appearance on *Strictly Come Dancing,* is hardly conducive to a state of invisibility.

Harrogate is not without its places of historic interest and, as the pace of the group slowed to a mere gallop, I was desperate for further relief in the form of a museum, perhaps, where I was hoping I might find a sumptuous sofa in which to sit and admire the exhibits. To say that I was apoplectic when the group disappeared into a branch of Debenhams, to buy the group leader a throw for *his* sofa, would be to understate fact.

Jayne, Denise and me did discuss staging a mutiny but, being the strong confident women that we all are, we fell silently back into step behind the group once they had purchased their soft furnishing items instead. Our next destination, we were informed, was going to be a visit to Betty's tea rooms, to enjoy the delights of a cream tea. Not only had I little sensation remaining below my knees at this point, so the sight of a long queue snaking its way outside, the full length of the building, was bad enough, but I was, by now becoming desperate to be free of this alien experience and all the reasons that had propelled me towards it in the first place. Denise and Jayne joined me at the back of the queue and I happened to glance around the adjacent corner, which resulted in a timely and instant lift in my spirits. By using a series of covert hand signals, I was able to relay to Denise and Jayne my discovery of a sandwich board advertising two-for-one cocktails during happy hour which, by an equally happy coincidence, was just about to start. When we were satisfied that we would not be observed, we each disappeared around the corner and were soon installed in the comfortable seating outside the *Slug & Lettuce*, enjoying a Mojito. Our only remaining problem was how many of them we could consume before the half-price offer expired.

The cocktails flowed, as did the conversation. I already knew that Denise had been a teacher before her retirement, but I also learned that she was a very adventurous and well-travelled lady too. Jayne is also a very accomplished woman with a background that includes social services and project management but, when the conversation came round to me, I remember feeling very pale by comparison. My own *achievements* have owed much more to my ability to fly by the seat of my pants than anything else and I felt like a bit of a Del girl in the company I was in.

It is amazing how quickly an hour can slip by when consuming cocktails at the rate of two-for-one and how much easier the walk back to the hotel became because of them. However, our breakout from Betty's had not gone unnoticed and an unwelcoming committee was waiting for us back at the hotel who were clearly not impressed by our impromptu deviation from the itinerary. The three of us decided that now might be a good time to retreat to the sanctity of my room and, of course, the comforting contents of Denise's fridge.

The show must go on

Through our postings online, Denise and Jayne were both aware that a couple of months previously I had held a memorial party to celebrate all things Kenny and the wonderful life we shared together. For reasons not really clear to me at the time, I had decided that I would make a short film to show during it, which I had brought with me to share with them.

When I look back now, with the all-important benefit of hindsight, I can easily see the defining moments in the process of my own grieving though, as I have said repeatedly, they certainly were not evident as such at the time. The inspiration for the film came to me in the form of a quote taken from a sonnet by a Chilean poet called Pablo Neruda, sent to me by one of the ladies on Widow World, though I am quite sure that Tina, the lady who sent it and who I have since had the very great pleasure of meeting, could never have guessed as to the impact that the following few words would have on me. I often said that Kenny had the soul of a poet, even though his expressive capabilities were far more basic Mancunian than lyrical, but I knew in an instant when I read the following exactly why it had been given to me.

Legacy of love – Pablo Neruda

'If I die survive me with such pure force you make the pallor and the coldness rage; flash your indelible eyes from south to south, from sun to sun, till your mouth sings like a guitar. I don't want your laugh or your footsteps to waver; I don't want my legacy of happiness to die'.

I was deeply ashamed now of my *cunning plan*, which was the antithesis of all that Kenny had wanted for me, and I suppose the film, essentially a collage of our most precious memories, was my way of showing him that now I understood my responsibility to preserve his legacy of happiness. Having said that, my IT skills, though improving slowly, had not yet been tested by the vagaries of my editing suite and, this meant, that footage was inclined to appear on the website page of a bewildered bloke in Bangkok with depressing regularity. My task was made no easier by the fact that it was Kenny who had been the cinematographer in our house, and he left literally hundreds of hours of video for me to trawl through. Spending so many hours with the vibrant larger-than-life images of my husband, and hearing his voice every day, was much more of a challenge than I expected, not least because I knew that, when the film was finally finished, I would have to learn to be without him all over again.

The party

The day of the party arrived and, as per usual where I am concerned, was not without its fair degree of drama, even though I do try very hard to dot the T's and cross the I's?

The party was held in a plush local hotel and, a couple of hours before our guests were due to arrive, I thought it a good idea to go and check on the progress of the preparations so far. I was delighted to see that the room had been decorated in accordance with my wishes, with lots of red balloons in recognition of Kenny's lifelong support of his beloved Manchester United. These were interspersed with the sky blue colour of Manchester City, to ensure that those of us on the other side of the city's famous footballing divide were also fairly represented.

On each table, there was a hat for every one of our guests. Kenny loved to wear hats of all different types which, for a bald guy who liked to spend most of his free time in Florida, was probably quite fortuitous. Also on the tables were bottles of Babycham and cans of an American beer especially imported from the US for the occasion. I explained to Denise and Jayne the significance of the drinks and how my sixteen-year-old self-had considered Babycham to be the very height of sophistication when Kenny ordered it for me on our very first date. It was to be an illusion without longevity, though, when after two of them I quickly assumed the gait of a new-born deer taking its first few steps on a frozen pond, after which Kenny nicknamed me Bambi. The beer was something that my husband had acquired a taste for on our first few trips to Florida when our finances allowed us to travel there but not much else. Despite the fact that this was a beer that taste had forgotten, on account of the fact that it was justifiably very, very cheap, Kenny persevered with it in his quest to eke out our meagre budget. Later, when our financial constraints eased and we could afford an upgrade to a better brand, he wouldn't hear of it, saying that the taste of cheap American beer reminded him not just of the many happy holidays we had enjoyed there, but also of how far we had come since those early trips.

Satisfied that everything appeared to be going to plan and, on seeing that the DJ had arrived to begin the preparation for his set, I asked a member of staff to help me hook up my laptop to the in-house system, in readiness for the premiere of my very first film production. I wasn't too worried at first when it became obvious that the connections on my fairly new laptop were not compatible with the hotel's equipment, as I had been assured they would be. I just assumed that I would be directed to a solution to the problem. I was indeed given several suggestions on how to resolve the issue, and the best of these is indicative of the quality of some of the others. I was advised to put my laptop onto a stool, and then to further elevate this arrangement by placing the whole ensemble on top of a table, so that its fourteen-inch screen could then be squinted at by all of those in the room. Furthermore, when I turned the volume up to its fullest capacity, this would also mean that anyone sitting in very close proximity to it would actually be able to hear it too. I only stopped laughing at the point when I realised that no one else was and that this was a solution offered in all seriousness.

After all the hard work I had put into the film I was distraught at the prospect of not being able to show it as planned. I demanded to see the booking manager, who I was then reliably informed had booked off for the evening. This information caused the volume of my protests to increase dramatically and to become peppered with some of the rarer examples of Anglo Saxon expletives.

Curious as to the cause of the commotion, the DJ explained that he could lend me an older laptop whose connections were compatible with the in-house system. If I could find something to transfer the film from my laptop onto his, it would be possible to use the large screen and audio as originally planned. An idea popped into my head which had the potential to solve the dilemma and, if I was right, it would be provided by Kenny himself. My late husband had form for being able to produce the most unlikely item at exactly the point of its greatest need and, as I quickly rifled through the bags of his camera equipment which I had brought with me to film the event, I could only hope that the small matter of his demise would not prevent him from doing so again. Finally, my fingers alighted on a memory stick tucked away in a side pocket – problem solved.

I was so grateful for the intervention of the DJ and, helped by the relaxing effects of a couple of drinks, I was unable to be dissuaded from expressing the depths of that gratitude, by giving him a sum of money that would easily have covered the cost of private education for at least one his children. Unfortunately, because of the emotional roller coaster that I had been on for most of the day and the effects of alcohol, the memory stick was the only item of Kenny's photographic equipment that was put to any use that evening. Perhaps this was Kenny's way of telling me, now that our precious memories had been recorded and shared, the time had come for me to start creating brand new ones to live alongside them.

As Denise, Jayne and I watched the film together, locked in a mutual understanding that is mercifully unavailable to those who have not experienced losing their spouse or partner, there were, of course, more than a few tears shed that afternoon. The last frame of the film features nothing other than the sound of Kenny laughing hysterically as he was so often inclined to do which, thankfully, was enough to persuade our smiles to return and was another affirmation of the adage that laughter really is the best medicine. Denise reminded me that I had once referred to all of us as GOWNS in a post on Widow World and asked me what I had meant by it. To be honest, I could barely remember having done so but, not for the first time and thinking on my feet, replied that it had been an acronym for Grieving Overwhelmed Widows Negotiating Stuff. This was, perhaps, the moment when the first green shoots of an idea began to emerge.

Once more unto the breach

Not really knowing what to expect of dinner or the rest of the evening, Denise, Jayne and I put our best feet forward and were determined to try harder to engage with the other members of the group. Dinner, whilst palatable enough, was otherwise pretty unremarkable and by dessert I was fighting off the effects of an afternoon spent drinking cocktails, followed by more drinks from Denise's fridge, wine over dinner, and the soporific effects of the food. Once having taken delivery of my lemon meringue I couldn't decide whether I should eat it or sleep on it. Eventually, people began to migrate towards the lounge bar, and

I reluctantly ordered a lemonade in an attempt to retain the ability to speak in full sentences, though, as it turned out, I might as well have ordered a large vodka instead.

Taking a deep breath, I took a seat by the side of a lady who appeared to be on the outer fringes of a group, who were all heavily engaged in conversation. My initial greeting was warm and friendly, but my backside had barely hovered over the velvet pile on the chair beneath it before I was asked how long it had been for me. This question, in the context of the company I was in, simply refers to the length of time that had elapsed since my loss and was not one I would have expected to encounter during the first conversation in any other circumstance. If I thought, however, that it was a precursor to discovering something about me, then I was to be very quickly dispossessed of any such notion. I answered that it had been eight months since I had lost Kenny, but the words had hardly left my lips before I was informed that it had been almost ten years for my companion. I was then assured that a mere eight months was hardly long enough for me to register the fact that my husband hadn't just nipped out to the local shops, instead of the cemetery. This was followed by several questions in quick succession but, after the first two, I realised that answers were simply not required. I retreated into the depths of my chair and listened politely to the explicit details of her husband's illness and subsequent death all of which was delivered in a style reminiscent of Les Dawson's Ada Sidebottom. I was actually quite saddened that this poor lady seemed to be far more comfortable with the events of her past than she was about engaging in the present.

Hoping that a pregnant pause might be imminent, I held up my long empty glass of lemonade and signalled my intention to rectify this with a visit to the bar – but my gesture was in vain. Caught like a rabbit in a headlight, I was yet to learn how this lady's mother wanted to visit her son-in-law for one last time so had requested that he send her the money to buy a train ticket. This he flatly refused to do, on account of the fact that they had never see eye to eye, and he saw no reason for her to put in an appearance now that he was on his death bed. Determined that she would be not deprived of her opportunity to have the last word, the old lady set out on her train journey regardless, only to learn on arrival that her nemesis had passed away during it. An act, which my companion firmly believed, was a last and deliberate one of spite on his part, designed to avoid paying for the train ticket. By now I was genuinely scared at the prospect of becoming this lady in another nine years' time and resolved then and there to do everything in my power to avoid this particular fate.

If the Pablo Neruda quote had come my way quite by chance, then so had a book called *Second Firsts* by Christina Rasmussen and, once again, the Widow World site was instrumental in this. One of the contributors had been reading my posts on the site for some time and is a delightful lady, if a little shy, so posted only occasionally herself. She came across Christina's book and said that, after reading it, she felt compelled to recommend it to me. I was intrigued and, not for the first time, I turned to the services of Amazon and read the book from cover to cover in less than a couple of hours after it was delivered. Christina Rasmussen is an American author who had written about the stages of grief in her professional capacity as a counsellor, prior to the death of her husband in 2006, after which her beliefs and insights changed dramatically. In her book, she talks about a number of concepts, and I related to many of them, but it was her description of the *waiting room* that resonated with me the most.

The *waiting room*, Christina tells us, is a safe place into which the bereaved retreat in order to process their grief and consider what to do next. She then goes on to explain how some people can become stuck within the confines of this safe place because the familiarity of their loss, eventually, becomes less scary to them than the prospect of leaving it.

As I looked around the room and politely made my excuses to the lady by my side, who had been talking at me now for nearly an hour, I was convinced more than ever that Christina's theory concerning the existence of the *waiting room* was absolutely valid.

A brief glance in the direction of Denise and Jayne revealed facial expressions that confirmed that they too were having experiences, not unlike my own. I headed towards an empty chair in the corner of the bar, hoping for a moment's solitude, but was promptly intercepted, with all the speed and precision of the Green Lantern, by another widow keen to relate the story of her loss. Fearing the worst and hoping for the best, I dutifully replied that it had been eight months, in response to the inevitable question, until the sound of someone skilfully running their fingers over the keys of a grand piano, suddenly cut a welcome swathe through the gloom in the room. I turned to see who was responsible for the medley of familiar tunes emanating from the piano, half hoping that this gesture might alert my present company to a shift in my listening preferences.

The pianist was joined by a lady whose enthusiastic attempts at singing along more than made up for the fact that she quite possibly qualified for the services of a hearing dog. Soon, quite a few other members of the group were joining in too. I began to dare hope that there might be some enjoyment to be had during this evening after all. The welcome diversion, however, was not destined to last, when a member of the hotel staff received a complaint from a resident concerning the noise, which resulted in the issue of a cease and desist order.

As someone who has attended many live music events in her dim and distant past, I completely failed to see how this gentle form of entertainment, as tuneless as it may have been, could have been described in any way as noisy. The resultant silence was not unpopular with everyone, though, and the Green Lantern lady was quick to seize her chance to resume our conversation, after which I was reasonably confident that I would be capable of carrying out a minor surgical procedure without assistance.

The Widow World weekend was not a social event that I, or indeed Denise and Jayne, felt we would ever need to repeat if only because it had served to provide us with a glimpse of a future we all agreed would be unthinkable. We were grateful, though, to have had the opportunity to finally meet each other in person. As a few reflective minutes of silence were punctuated by the gentle whirring of Denise's fridge, we squeezed out the last few remaining drops of prosecco which, though greatly depleted in quantity, was still impressively cold, and raised our glasses to GOWNS and all those negotiations yet to come.

Chapter 5

Rough notes, sketches and little else

Meat on the bones

After Harrogate, Jayne, Denise and I continued to post on Widow World though, by now, the entity that was becoming Grieving Overwhelmed Widows Negotiating Stuff, or GOWNS, was much more in evidence. We continued to talk about all of our various negotiations which included the smallest of things, like learning to shop for one, to those such as the purchase of a new car or home. As usual, we told our stories from a humorous perspective, which seemed to be appreciated in general and especially by those of us who had suffered our losses within a similar time frame. It did start to concern me, though, how the newer members logging onto the forum for the first time might regard our tendency to laugh at each other, and ourselves, as somehow trivialising the grieving process. It occurred to me that it might be more appropriate to create something more specifically geared towards the

GOWNS ethos. I thought that this might be achieved by creating a purpose-built website but, as for how this might be brought about, I had no idea given my under-developed technical knowhow, which meant that my ideas at this time were confined to a few rough notes, sketches and very little else.

The next time that Jayne, Denise and I met up was during another weekend, this time in Scarborough, only now we were free of the confines of the group mentality that had dominated much of our stay in Harrogate. The unreliable British weather was on our side for a change and Jayne suggested a trip to the forest of Dalby so that we could take full advantage of it. More like children, and not the senior members of society that we undoubtedly are, we dipped our toes in a quaint little brook which meandered under the shady apron of some ancient trees. Actually, that is not strictly accurate: whilst Denise and Jayne, who were both wearing flip flops, an item of footwear that I will never understand and certainly will never own, were soon rolling up their trousers, I wasn't about to untie the lovely white ribbons lacing up my flat (a well-remembered lesson from Harrogate) but still superbly sparkly pumps, in favour of a quick paddle over some pebbles in a puddle, however picturesque it might have been.

If I do say so myself my own inbuilt navigation system is actually quite impressive, but when, after a lovely day relaxing in the forest, Jayne decided that we would use an alternative route back to Scarborough, I was happy to defer to her judgement, given that she is familiar with the area and I am not. Chatting away happily, and enjoying the scenic route we were embarked upon, even if the road was becoming more and more like a track as we progressed further along it, Jayne continued to insist that, despite this, we were still going in the right direction. I was beginning to think that there was a much greater likelihood that we would bump into Bilbo Baggins ahead of the toilet that Denise was now suggesting her need of was becoming quite urgent. I popped in a CD to try and take her mind off her nether regions, which seemed to do the trick, as the enquiries concerning our distance from the nearest toilet appeared to stop. Then I noticed that they had been replaced by what sounded suspiciously like stifled sobbing.

The strains of *'You'll Never Walk Alone'* emanating from the CD player had been a particular favourite song of Denise's late husband, Jim, and, of course, had caused one of those tsunami moments we are all familiar with. Apologising profusely, I quickly skipped several tracks at random to select another song, only to observe Jayne's face crumple this time as I inadvertently managed to replace one tear-jerker with another.

A cursory glance at the fuel gauge identified another potential problem, other than being deep inside a forest with two widows, one of whom was already wet at one end and threatening to be the same at the other. Jayne hadn't been able to see her way out of our predicament, even before she became blinded by tears, so I decided on direct action and took over navigating our way back to civilisation, petrol and a suitable source of relief for Denise.

Over fish and chips in Whitby that weekend, the three of us talked in-depth about my ideas for GOWNS and how we might bring some of them to fruition. Both Denise and Jayne are far more technically savvy than I, so it wasn't long before they were able to convince me that the creation of a GOWNS website might not be as difficult as I had previously imagined. Whilst Denise loved the ideas for a website, and wanted very much to be involved, she is a very busy lady who still travels as much as she ever did, even learning to tow her own caravan after the advent of her seventieth birthday, so the demands on her time are huge. Ever grateful for Denise's help and early input, Jayne and I began the process of creating a website, and the following paragraph is taken directly from those rough notes I had written when the ideas for it were just about beginning to take shape.

'The ambient nature of the site should be positive and upbeat, using humour extensively, but with a caution that this approach might not be suitable for everyone. The site does not seek to advise or counsel but is simply a place in which to explore the use of humour during the process of grieving and how this can prove beneficial for some'.

Gowns: The influences – Jayne Benge

The following was written by Jayne shortly after we started to think about how we could bring our ideas for GOWNS to life.

'The online community was a place I felt I could bear my soul during the darkest time in my life. I was amongst a collective of people who were all allowed to say 'we know how you feel' because they did.

I am by nature, a person who tries very hard to have a glass half full attitude towards life and, have always had a good sense of humour, so when I started to see posts on the site from a fellow member who created a cocktail of wisdom and humour, I knew I had found a kindred spirit. I couldn't help but smile at Sandra's stories and felt compelled to join in, and by doing so, was learning how to deal with my feelings of grief. It became obvious to me that for many people, even in their darkest place, they all still feel uplifted by humour.

When I eventually met up with Sandra and got to know her personally, we connected on many levels, of which, humour was key. There comes a time in the period of our grieving when we allow ourselves guilt-free laughter and smiles. We accept that we will always have tears of joy and tears of sadness, but for GOWNS we want the tears of joy to kick the butt of the tears of sadness. We want to share stories that will make us smile, we want to shove the stigma where it belongs, and feel we have a place to go where we can guarantee to feel uplifted. Sandra and I were drawn together through humour and we know we have to share it.'

It is still a source of huge fascination to me that, whilst I was oblivious to it, Jayne's own journey towards widowhood had started around the same time as my own and, as she lives in Hull some seventy-odd or so miles from me, it is unlikely that our paths would ever have crossed in any other way than they did. No matter how many times I try and fathom the odds of us clicking buttons at the same point in time and, as a result, becoming the firm friends that we undoubtedly are today is, in my view, beyond mere coincidence.

Jayne is, in many ways, an archetypal Yorkshire lass, in that she is geographically predisposed to telling it like it is and possesses the calm sort of authority you know that you would be able to rely on in a crisis. Whilst we do share the same proclivity for straight-talking, it's probably fair to say that I might have a slightly more diplomatic edge, though it would be equally true to say that I am much more likely to be the cause of a crisis than someone you would want to help you navigate through one.

Jayne is both practical and logical, with areas of shade not particularly prevalent in her thinking. I, on the other hand, cannot even follow a recipe without altering it, planning very little in my life and inclined to go off at a tangent at any time. Things like spreadsheets also loom large in Jayne's ordered and organised world, and she has one of these for every conceivable scenario. I vividly remember the moment when she first introduced me to one, in an attempt to focus my attention in a more productive way. My shock on learning that they were a real organisational tool was completely genuine because I had so far imagined that a spreadsheet was some kind of Yorkshire witticism for toilet paper. Jayne will shop for necessities, considers B&Q to be her spiritual home and thinks that flip flops and builders boots are the epitomai of style and elegance, whereas I shop for shoes ahead of necessities, am genuinely scared and confused by all things related to DIY, and would rather amputate my own feet before wearing any of the aforementioned footwear.

Maybe it is these differences that make our partnership work as well as it does. In many ways, Jayne reminds me of Kenny, who knew exactly how to encourage my better ideas and, whilst he would never tell me directly when he thought I was way off beam, had a way of ensuring that my more outlandish ideas withered on the vine, as though at my own behest. If Kenny and I considered ourselves to be a double act, two halves of the same thing, then this was also true of Jayne and her late husband, Steve. A love of the comedic was the central plank on which both of our relationships were based, and that appreciation of humour was something we each recognised in the other, from our early posts on the Widow World forum, as Jayne herself has described.

When we did meet up to make our plans for GOWNS, our tendency to fall into an easy style of banter would often result in us laughing so hard that a change of underwear was necessary on a regular basis. Being able to laugh out loud again with someone who wouldn't automatically assume that this meant you must have *got over* losing your husband was quite liberating. Neither Jayne nor I felt the need to explain or apologise for daring to suggest that laughing was not an act incongruous with grief, because it really helped and we were the living proof that it did. The relationship between Jayne and myself began to quite naturally evolve into a new double act, by which stage we had started to do a lot of research into the physical and psychological benefits of laughter therapy, discovering that there was plenty of scientific research to confirm many of the benefits we knew that we had already experienced for ourselves.

Michael Rowe

We are each destined to meet many people throughout the course of our lives, with some of them leaving a greater impression on us than others. Michael Rowe, a teacher at my primary school when I was ten years old, was the person who taught me about tenacity. This quality can be both a blessing and a curse as I have alluded to earlier in this book, but it definitely helped me to survive the loss of my husband and to go on to create GOWNS with Jayne.

My recollection of Michael Rowe is still vivid, as though the fifty years that have elapsed since I saw him last could not possibly be the half a century that it is. He was a small, thick-set man who was always immaculately dressed. His dark raven black hair and beard were gently flecked with only the merest hint of grey, and his piercing blue eyes seemed to be capable of looking deep inside your very soul. He was a true English eccentric, who was inclined to extend the crook of his walking stick towards you before hooking it around your neck and drawing you close when he felt you needed the benefit of his advice particularly urgently.

I was regarded as a bright enough student but was often described as being *highly strung* and, whilst I had no understanding of what that was supposed to mean at the time, I do have a vague recollection of a doctor instructing my mother to pour the contents of a sachet into my mouth when necessary. I can't remember her ever having done so, and when I look back on some of the childcare practices of the 60's and 70's surviving them was no mean feat of achievement. If my mother chose to disregard the advice she was given, it was probably because she knew that, if I was inclined to act out on occasion, it was because the burden of her own health issues weighed heavily on my young shoulders at the time. Despite this, it was widely expected that I would pass my eleven plus, which I duly did, though I was not allowed to attend the local grammar school on account of my perceived temperamental unsuitability.

Michael Rowe was a teacher who challenged you to challenge yourself, and I remember wanting to show him just what I was capable of, more than any other teacher I have known before or since. I'm not quite sure why, because any praise from him was sparse and fleeting, though possibly valued all the more because of this. On one particular morning, he handed me an essay that he had marked and I was completely crestfallen to see that the A-plus I had been hoping for, was, in fact, a lowly grade C.

I paid little attention to Michael Rowe during the lesson that followed, as I struggled to understand what it was about my essay that was so bad. My surly demeanour had not gone unnoticed and I was called to the front of the class at the end of the lesson. When Michael Rowe asked me what was wrong. I suggested that he take another look at my essay because I didn't understand why it hadn't achieved a higher grade. Without speaking he carefully re-read my offering in its entirety then took out his red marker pen and replaced my C grade with a D before thanking me for pointing out his mistake. It was then that the red mist descended and my tendency towards a hysterical outburst took over. I flounced out of the classroom, shouting what I hoped was a really rude expletive that I had heard my father use once, but I didn't quite manage to make my exit complete before I was called back to the teacher's desk. I fully expected to be given hundreds of lines about the alternatives available to us concerning our choice of language but, instead, Michael Rowe fixed those steely eyes on mine and said:

"Failure is not to be feared for it feeds success and remembers also, that success does not always come to extraordinary people who achieve extraordinary things, but to ordinary people who achieve extraordinary things."

During my first year at Secondary Modern school I was finally offered a place at Bury Grammar school, which I promptly told them to stick up their arses because, by then, thanks to Michael Rowe, I understood that a D grade for something written in the middle of the night in a hospital waiting room was, in fact, a fair reflection of its worth and, if I was ever going to create anything extraordinary from the ordinary, then I could do that from wherever I happened to be.

The laughter reflex

My earliest memory of what I now like to call the laughter reflex goes back to the days of my childhood and our visits to Blackpool. Even now, as my sixtieth year lies in wait, I can still recall the wonderfully sweet smell of spun sugar as it was formed into pink candy floss and the noise made by the old seafront trams trundling along a thin metal track, with sparks flying from the electrical conductors overhead.

If it was Charles Dickens who created a sinister interpretation of the clown figure that has, in more recent times, been the version portrayed in horror films and in some elaborate internet hoaxes, then my memories of the slapstick humour of Charlie Cairoli, and his collection of bumbling stumbling companions at the Tower Circus, were altogether more innocent. I laughed like a drain when a bucket of paper pieces was thrown into the audience, as a last-minute replacement for the water we were convinced would soak us all to our skins. Similarly, I found the laughing clown sitting at a jaunty angle on a throne by the entrance to the pleasure beach impossible to resist. I would stand next to his glass case laughing my head off for no other reason than he was and, on each and every occasion that I did, I was soon joined by people similarly infected with the giggling germ because there is no doubt that the mere sound of laughter is highly contagious.

Years later, at the tender age of eighteen and already running my first hairdressing business located within a Jewish community just outside of Manchester, it was traditional for the ladies to prepare chopped and fried fish on Friday mornings in time for the Shabbat meal later that day. Now I love chopped and fried fish, but the creation of it creates a rather pungent smell which permeates all that it comes into contact with. The application of warm water to the hair of those who have prepared this dish helps to release an aroma, not unlike that found at Billingsgate on a busy day.

On one particular Friday morning, my dear late mother came to the salon to help out on reception, something she did occasionally but, until then, never on a Friday. She was completely unaware, therefore, that the strong smell of fish was not because of a fault with the electrics, which apparently is a recognised indication that there might be, so she was soon on all fours systematically sniffing the plug sockets and advising my clientele, who were themselves blissfully immune to the smell, to prepare to evacuate the building. Thankfully, I was able to intercept my mother just as she was about to break the glass in the fire alarm and discreetly explain to her the real reason for the smell. Probably to help hide her embarrassment my mother was soon engulfed by an uncontrollable fit of giggling, which rendered her incapable of any explanation as to the source of her amusement. For sound business reasons, I was not about to provide an explanation either, and soon the whole salon broke out into a riotous uproar though, until now, no one else other than my mother and I knew why. I give you the laughter reflex more contagious than glandular fever and much more fun.

Fake it till you make it

During our research into using laughter as a therapy Jayne and I learned that, even when laughter is not as a response to something amusing, the exact same benefits apply when our laughter is faked. We decided, therefore, that we needed to learn the techniques used to illicit fake, as opposed to real, laughter.

The moment we met laughing John Hipkiss, our tutor on a laughter therapy facilitation course was not one that I will readily forget. Whilst it is quite usual for a greeting to include a firm handshake and a ready smile, a sudden and unexpected bout of raucous laughter, directed just inches away from your nose, was much less usual. Not quite sure what to make of such an introduction, I resorted to a nervous giggle, for which John immediately offered me his congratulations, followed by a hearty slap on the back. I looked towards Jayne, whose expression at this point was of the horrible type you tend to adopt when you suspect that a sudden episode of explosive diarrhoea might be imminent. When we had both recovered sufficiently we decided that the amount we had paid to learn how to fake laughter was too large an investment to forgo, so we introduced ourselves to the rest of the group, more than a little apprehensive as to what might happen next.

Our fellow classmates were a diverse and interesting mix of people, whose reasons for wanting to learn how laughter as a therapy could be applied were spread over a variety of fields, such as education and lifestyle, in our case bereavement, and one lady whose aim was simply to reconnect with her inner child.

Throughout the course, John showed us a variety of exercises which were designed to show us the many ways in which laughter can be faked. We pretended to be petrol lawnmowers, for instance and, in order to start our engines, we were encouraged to laugh quietly at first, gradually working on both the volume and velocity of our guffaws until they represented an engine functioning at the fullness of its capacity, after which we trotted along behind these imaginary machines, pretending to cut grass.

Quite frankly, if the purpose of this exercise was to produce fake laughter, mine was absolutely twenty-four carat the genuine article which, of course, made me worry that, in this particular context, I might be regarded as something of a fraud. Despite the surreal nature of the activities, Jayne and I persevered with the exercises and, as the group began to bond, we all became far more comfortable and less self-conscious than we had been at the start. At the end of the course, we were asked to produce a shortened version of a laughter therapy session by ourselves, using what we had learned and introducing new ideas of our own. As per usual, my imagination ran on ahead in a way that demonstrated my own inner child never lurks any deeper than just below the surface, whilst Jayne concentrated on making something that was workable in the time we had been allocated. Pleased with what we had learned, and imagining many ways that we could improve on it, Jayne and I both became qualified laughter therapy facilitators. Throughout our time with laughing John we had been part of, and witnessed at first hand, the way in which the unifying power of laughter had crossed, without effort, the divides of background, class and culture, and we were more convinced than ever that this was something that should lie at the very heart of GOWNS.

The GOWNS website

When Jayne and I created the GOWNS website some three years ago, the idea of using laughter and humour in the field of grief was not as readily accepted as it has become since. We were keen that users of the site would be able to see in an instant that this was a place where we understood grief but chose to use laughter and humour as a way of dealing with it. We always envisioned our site as being interactive through a dedicated forum, but we soon found that the templates we had to work with were cumbersome and in no way equipped to compete with the speed and accessibility of social media sites such as Facebook, which are easily understood and used globally. In recognition of this Jayne, created a GOWNS closed group on Facebook so that our members who want to, can converse there, safe in the knowledge that only other members have access to the things that they want to share. Sometimes GOWNS feel unable to express themselves freely, for a variety of reasons when they think that their posts might be seen by friends or family members.

The launch of the GOWNS website

Jayne and I launched our website on the 9th of June 2016 or, to be more precise, we missed the launch of our website on that date. Just what we were expecting might happen when a website went live was not entirely clear to either of us at the time. We did agree, however, that an ice bucket and a bottle of champagne were probably appropriate, as we waited to see if our laptops would light up like Las Vegas fruit machines in notification of the exact moment of the launch. The reality of the situation was that we both received e-mails from friends, congratulating us on the site, well ahead of us realising that our baby's entrance into the world had been achieved without so much as a push from either of us. We were determined to be much more efficient when it came to wetting its head, so promptly supped the champagne and headed for the nearest pub to celebrate. If on the 10th June 2016 we both woke up with hangovers, we did at least have a website of which we are justifiably very proud.

GOWNS on film

I am a bit of a show-off. I don't mean to be and put it down to the frustrated thespian that has always lurked within me, probably from a very young age. If there was a stage production at school, I wanted to be in it and was never going to be content with making up the numbers in a group of extras – it was centre stage or nothing. My inability to stick to a script usually meant that the production we had rehearsed bore little to no resemblance to the one that was performed in front of an audience because I could never resist the chance of raising a chuckle with a bit of timely improvisation. Then there is Jayne, bless her, who, for reasons of her own, actually had quite an aversion to being filmed when we first met.

My suggestion that we should introduce ourselves to our members of GOWNS during a short film and, after this, we should similarly document all of our latest negotiations was enough to remove the colour from Jayne's cheeks far more quickly than her usual Brillo pad ever could. Perhaps, it was the film I created for Kenny's memorial that was the original prompt behind this idea sometimes it is easier to show people who are grieving that it's OK to laugh, rather than just telling them.

It was also important to try and break down the common stereotypes that I talk about in the introduction to this book but, whatever the rationale that lay behind our cinematic efforts, and even if they didn't make one single person laugh, then the two of us more than made up for it when making them. I got to show off big time and Jayne is no longer inclined to hide behind the sofa when the camera comes out. Some of our members have even posted their own efforts on our Facebook Group and this, in my view, is a brilliant way of getting to know the person behind the posts and texts, which often don't say the things that we really want them to, or show us as the people we really are behind the masks we tend to adopt whilst grieving.

It is often said that the only certainty in life is death and, as GOWNS, we know only too well how it feels be in Christina Rasmussen's *waiting room*. I can, however, state with a degree of certainty that I laughed before I went into that *waiting room*, a good chunk of the time I was in there, and I'm laughing outside of it again too.

Chapter 6

The negotiations

Living for one

I n the weeks before Kenny died, when I remained largely in denial that he would, there were a few moments when I did allow myself to try out a few widow manoeuvres, in the vain hope that I could somehow prepare myself if the worst should happen. In truth, it didn't matter how many times I practised saying out loud that I had lost my husband to cancer, or how many times I sat alone in a hospital canteen during his treatments and pretended that this was how it would feel if he died, in reality losing someone you love so completely causes a degree of pain for which there is no adequate plan of preparation.

It is often the simplest of things that can bring you to your knees when you least expect them to. There is that moment when you browse the aisles of a supermarket and automatically turn to your husband to ask what he fancies for tea, and then you remember that you will never hear his response to that question ever again. As a direct consequence of this, you now find yourself forced into the *cooking for one* negotiation. Given that my late husband's idea of a gastronomic adventure was either a bacon or sausage sandwich, I had now, at least, gained the dubious advantage of autonomy in my gastronomical choices, only to discover that food manufacturers do not recognise consumers in units of less than two. Before my husband's death, I was prolific in the kitchen, though my love of culinary creation pretty much died with him.

As previously documented, I survived initially on a diet of corn which, interestingly enough, when liquefied, turns into Smirnoff. Later when I re-introduced solids back into my diet which, at that stage, usually came out of a tin or a packet, it often meant that the stringent pong of a half-eaten meal for two, or the odour of the forgotten four of a tin of six hot dogs, was the first thing to greet me on opening my fridge door. Thankfully, my previous life as something of a foodie had equipped me well enough to realise that these new arrangements were neither a healthy or cost-effective option in the long term, so I worked hard at reducing my over-reliance on liquid corn and convenience foods in that precise order.

It would be wrong, however, to assume that I experienced some kind of epiphany. There was no sudden U-turn back to the days when boxes of organic fruit and veg would appear on my front doorstep on a regular basis, nor was my freezer filled with everything from curried goat to spotted dick in anticipation of the four-minute warning. I think it was more the case that I had reached a new stage in the process of my grieving, where I realised that my own sustenance was important after all, but I was unable to nurture this need in the ways of old, because they were becoming irrelevant to the newer version of me that was slowly emerging. Gradually I learned to make healthy choices when I felt able and managed to stop beating myself up when the lapses occurred because I was beginning to find other uses for the time that I would otherwise have spent in the kitchen.

The things that change in the lives of widows and widowers can be summed up in just one word – EVERYTHING. The full extent and scope of those changes, though, are far from obvious at first; rather they reveal themselves over time. Married couples, or those in long term partnerships, inevitably settle into their own roles within their relationships and, usually, everyday household tasks are divided between them. When Kenny died I was catapulted into an alien realm where things like fuses, lawnmowers, and light bulbs of all shapes, sizes and flavours resided. I was reduced to tears on many an occasion when I couldn't perform the simplest of tasks, which left me with no choice but to hand over fist's full of cash to a variety of people to do them for me, with all the financial implications that come with this. Re-learning old experiences from a new perspective is not an easy negotiation.

The Occasion Negotiation

The occasion negotiation is another example of how the familiar milestones in life change after the loss of a spouse or partner. At the time of writing I have experienced several Christmases as a widow; negotiated a birth – not me personally, I hasten to add, but a new addition to the family; birthdays; anniversaries; and a wedding.

My first Christmas alone came only a few months after Kenny died and, still protected by the phenomenon that is widow brain, I quite fancied that I could create a Christmas that would be much like the ones that had preceded it. I learned quickly and painfully that I could not.

The advertising moguls would have us believe that having a new sofa delivered before Christmas, possibly a new Smart TV and food purchased from the big three supermarkets anytime from September onwards, in quantities that would solve the problem of the world's starving populations, is somehow essential to the enjoyment of Christmas. The actual reality was that, due to my overindulgence in Morrison's mince pies and Christmas spirit, I was sick all over the new sofa and couldn't even see the Smart TV, let alone appreciate its level of artificial intelligence. No amount of glitter or twinkling Christmas lights could change the fact that Christmas, as I had known it, was now firmly a part of my past. Determined to do things differently the following year, I spent the whole of Christmas day dressed in an oversized reindeer *Onesie* and microwaved anything that needed serving hot straight from the packets of prepared food I had bought from Marks and Spencer. I didn't enjoy Christmas that year either but, at least, I had started to recognise that the occasion negotiation would continue to come round, much like a hamster on a wheel, and it was up to me to now to find a new and different way of celebrating it.

The Travel Negotiation

All relationships have different sets of priorities and, for Kenny and I, working to fund our frequent trips to Florida lay at the heart of ours. This was also true of Jayne and Steve too though, as Jayne is not a fan of flying long distances, their destinations of choice tended to be more European, where Jayne could also be sure that she would be unlikely to run into a mouse wearing clothes, or be mown down by a typical burger-eating American, spilling out from the confines of a disability scooter – her words, not mine!

As alluded to earlier, there is much about meeting Jayne that has transcended the boundaries of coincidence and the fact that we ended up negotiating our first trip abroad without our husbands was not a deliberate plan, but it is exactly what happened nonetheless. If the party island of Ibiza is not an obvious choice of holiday destination for two middle-aged widows, this is quite simply because it wasn't. Thinking that I might prefer to try on a pair of Ugg boots in public rather than agree to go to Ibiza with some friends to check out a wedding venue, I felt obliged at the time to nod in mute agreement instead. I was assured that my accommodation in Ibiza for the five-day duration of our trip was of the five-star all-inclusive kind, this on account of the fact that no one wants to spend five minutes with me, let alone five days if I am unhappy with my surroundings. I admit I do have form for the odd diva strop on the rare occasions that this has happened and, whilst I had never been all-inclusive anywhere before, I was reasonably hopeful that I would be able to cope with it in the short term.

Of course, it had been Jayne who had borne the brunt of my continual complaining about having to go on the trip in the first place when, without warning, one of my friends was not able to travel, which meant that there was now a spare ticket going begging. I immediately thought of asking Jayne if she would like it – there was no doubt in my mind that the opportunity for us to negotiate our first flights without our husbands, together, would be good for both of us. The problem was that I had spared Jayne none of the gory details when it came to voicing my fears about going to Ibiza. These included being force-fed ecstasy tablets, even when out shopping, becoming blinded by lasers or rendered deaf by music that could, in my opinion, have been a breach of the trades description act to even describe it as such. As a consequence, I had left myself with something of a hard sell.

I concentrated on promoting the few remaining positives that I had not completely destroyed and pinned my hopes on the fact that that the hotel was in very close proximity to the beach, which I hoped might appeal to a water baby like Jayne, and, thankfully, this did prove to be the clincher.

Jayne is not an early riser so this time it was her turn to moan when she learned that we needed to get up in the middle of the night in order to be on time for our early flight. Gluten-free Strongbow, when consumed in the very wee small hours, is quite useful when you are dealing with a grumpy travelling companion, though Jayne made me promise that I would go swimming with her when we got to the resort, before agreeing to drink it. When extracting this promise, Jayne knew full well that my preference is for getting wet on the inside, as opposed to the outside. Later, in the course of honouring my agreement with her, I neglected to check the whereabouts of my phone. Twenty minutes after floating around the pool I realised that it was in the back pocket of my shorts which meant that I was firmly cut off from the outside world for the duration of our stay.

When the plane finally lifted from the tarmac at Manchester and propelled us towards the shores of Ibiza the tears were inevitable and spilt freely in testament to our memories but, they also represented a deep sense of pride too. Despite the fact that, until fairly recently, Jayne and I had been totally unaware of the existence of the other, together we were already achieving much than we ever thought would be possible.

The House for Sale Negotiation

Some of the negotiations we encounter as widows, widowers and those who have lost long-term partners are more complex to negotiate than others and my decision to sell the house which had been our family home for twenty odd years was an example of one of the most difficult. The house itself was much larger than I needed in terms of space now that I was alone and the cost of maintaining it would eventually have proved to be prohibitive too. Added to this was the emotional cost because, by now, I was struggling to live in the environment of my old life, whilst at the same time wanting to explore new experiences and widen my horizons in the life that I was slowly learning to inhabit. The sale of my house was agreed just days before I was due to undertake another travel negotiation, this time to Las Vegas. I write more extensively about this adventure in my next book, concerning the experiences of widows on internet dating sites. As is my usual practice, I largely ignored anything related either to my house move, or the up and coming trip to the US, until I reached the point at which this was no longer possible. The following are excerpts of posts I wrote for GOWNS when I realised that I could no longer ignore the necessary logistics required to move from one house to another.

4th May 2016

'Ooookay people...Just when I think that the lunatic pace of my life could not get any more frantic, it does exactly that. As you all know I am off to the states next week and my packing problems persist in that, I can't decide which bits of the clothes and shoe mountain will actually make the suitcase cut, but suffice to say that there will be casualties.
If packing for a two-week trip is proving to be beyond my capabilities at present, then quite how I will cope when it comes to packing up a large house and moving to something (yet to be discovered, but definitely something smaller) is anybody's guess.

I have this week accepted an offer on my house. I am now ready to wake up somewhere else and leave our lovely home to a new family, who I hope, will make their own memories within walls which have already seen so much fun and laughter during our watch.

My house purchaser's surveyor has been booked before I fly out to Vegas and, though there is little I can do to influence what he may or may not discover on a structural level, I can at least see to it that he has easy access to all areas, which might earn me the odd Brownie point. I did briefly consider exploring the space beneath the eaves in our loft room but was soon distracted by a trip to the shops to buy Bonjela, flight socks and my favourite perfume for my trip instead.

On my return, I pensively opened the sliding doors covering the eaves fully expecting that the hoarding nature of my late husband might reveal a few surprises but, I suspect that being able to see the sky outside from inside a cupboard and not through a window, would have been a surprise even to him. I closed the sliding doors much more quickly than I had opened them and consigned what I had seen behind them, into a file labelled forgotten.

I have also realised that now might be a good time to start to think a bit more about finding somewhere else to live. Watch this space folks! The following is an account of the first house that I viewed on my own.

16th July 2016

'Ooookay people... I think I might have got myself in a bit of a predicament, nothing too shocking in this I guess as chaos and I are pretty good pals already. I have decided that becoming homeless has little to recommend it and, in an attempt to avoid it, have finally been to view a house yesterday. I have been driving past it for some months now and have vaguely

entertained the idea that I might like to live in it. The house is offered with vacant possession, my vernacular at the moment is heavily peppered with such phrases.

I was greeted at the house by a cheery estate agent, who pointed out a bowl of rice sitting in the porch and commented on the fact that this was an odd place for it to be. Now we have already established that my understanding of anything building or DIY related would take up little room on the reverse side of a postage stamp, but even I didn't think that the rice was there for any other reason than to absorb excess moisture.

We proceeded into what could become my new living room if only I had no particular fondness for furniture. Admittedly, I do have rather a lot of it in my current home, so an opportunity to revise this would have been no bad thing, however, I do occasionally enjoy sitting down which I would be unable to do in this house unless I was prepared to do so on a perching stool.

I looked out of the front window into those facing directly opposite, a vista in direct contrast to the countryside one I currently enjoy, though which is sometimes punctuated by the sight of cows having a 'cuddle,' or at least this is how I explain this particularly amorous activity to my grandsons. I wondered briefly given the close proximities of the bedroom windows opposite how I would explain to them, a similar activity when carried out by humans.

The open plan kitchen? Well this area was more open than planned that's for sure, there was no room for my lovely range cooker and even though I tend to eat out of packets currently, and don't really need such an impressive appliance, I am not quite ready to use something that would need to be no bigger than the size of a Bunsen burner either.

A patio door lead into the tiny amount of 'outside space' something I have always called a garden or a back yard, but then I am not an estate agent. As we climbed the stairs, a feature I could have easily dispensed with in favour of one level living, I was further underwhelmed by a clutch of bedrooms which would require you to sleep whilst standing up. So what did viewing this house teach me? Well, I knew that compromises on space would be inevitable, I just hadn't realised on what scale given that this house is at the top of my budget. When I returned to my lovely home with all of its well thought out space and yes, all that flippin' furniture, I felt a little sad and more than a tad nauseous too. I know that this is the first house I have viewed and I might feel differently about the 'right one' when I meet it, but I am not as settled with my decision to move as I was. Do I stay or do I go? I think I'll go and pack for Vegas and try not to think about it for now'.

19th July 2016

'Ooookay people...today's negotiations have got off to a flyer as my house purchaser's surveyor arrived to do his thing earlier this morning. It has to be said that I am in quite a cheery mood at the moment as I anticipate the next two weeks in Vegas. Apart from the clothes and Shoe Mountain which still have yet to be culled and packed, I am no longer panicking in this respect. Instead, I am trying to adopt a Jayne type strategy, which basically involves the production of copious lists complete with approximate time scales for each outstanding task.

When I answered my door to a man holding onto his damp meter (he is definitely going to need one of those for sure) it was all I could do not to laugh out loud when I was confronted by what I can only describe as a Jason King lookalike albeit it, in miniature. I kid you not, this guy had enough facial hair to stunt double for Chewbacca and, his flared vintage trousers barely covered platform shoes that would not have looked out of place in the wardrobe of Elton John.

The surveyor expressed a preference for starting his examination at the top of the house and I bit my lip as my 'file under forgotten' strategy suddenly broke ranks and I remembered the daylight problem under the eaves. I watched as the spritely surveyor bounded up the staircase two at a time before disaster struck. His platform soles did not quite clear the top step, causing him to launch headfirst into the bedroom door adjacent to it. Unable to prevent an event in my shorts, I was relieved when the reassurances came that all was well, and I was free to try and locate something dry to wear. The only thing to hand was a dress I wear when colouring my hair and testament to this are many years of different coloured stains which cover most of the original fabric.

When Jason re-appeared he wanted to view my 'outside space' having attempted to disguise my tie-dye appearance, I stayed sitting behind my desk and gesticulated vaguely towards the kitchen where the backdoor keys could usually be found, though of course not on this occasion. I could see a slight twitch behind the facial hair as my change and choice of attire had not gone unnoticed when thankfully, I finally located the keys.

A few weeks before, and for the first time in my life, I did make an attempt to mow the lawn though not without consequences. Not realising that I needed to attach a grass box to the back of the mower to capture the cuttings, I had simply pushed the appliance over what used to be a lawn and the nettles that were successfully hidden in the undergrowth shot straight out of the back of the mower, ripping into my bare legs like shattered glass. I was more than a little pissed off when, in just over a week later, the grass was once again as high as an elephant's eye, and the nettles had *returned in force so I decided to just leave them to it, a decision I was now having some cause to regret.*

I could see that the surveyor was literally being held hostage in the garden by nettles that were threading their spiny tentacles deep into his polyester flared trousers, I shot back towards the sanctity of my desk and feigned ignorance of the poor man's predicament.

Once an escape from the garden had been effected, and the survey was completed I could only hope that my loose front door handle did not come off in my hand as it was often inclined to do just as I showed Jason out. Relieved that this time it stayed in place I exhaled deeply before spotting the damp meter which he had forgotten and explained why he was now banging on my door in the hope of retrieving his instrument. This time the front door handle proved to be less co-operative than before, which meant that I had no choice other than to force the meter through the letterbox in order to reunite it with its owner. I am utterly convinced that my property will likely be condemned. Being a member of GOWNS some day's people is definitely not for the faint-hearted'.

It was whilst I was negotiating the searing one hundred and twenty-degree heat in the Nevada desert that I received an e-mail confirming that, by some miracle, my purchasers were happy to continue to exchange of contracts after all. Thrilled and excited, I made a promise to my knees that I would find them a nice bungalow to live in as soon as I got back to the UK, but got distracted briefly by some fine-tasting wine in a Vegas casino and booked another trip instead, this time to Florida. This meant that I would be back in the UK for just seven days, during which time I would need to wash my knickers, re-pack them and find somewhere else to live, all before my departure.

My persistent searching of the internet eventually unearthed what looked to be a sweet little bungalow – not only was it in the right location but on sale at the right price too. The estate agents' pictures of the property showed that it was also in a walk-in condition which, for someone who hangs mirrors with blue tack, was a definite advantage.

Though convinced I had stumbled across just the thing I was looking for, I took the precaution of sending the property details to Jayne. Her ability to consider them objectively would not be influenced by such things as the colour of the front door or whether or not she liked the name of the street and the house number. Responding with her usual professionalism, Jayne's first query on receipt of my e-mail concerned the layout of the house. She asked me if I had looked at the floor plans, which of course I had not, in favour of musing over which items of my furniture would compliment the bungalow's existing scheme of décor.

Jayne flatly refused to engage with me in a conversation about soft furnishings until I agreed to go through the floor plans with her which, considering that I had asked for her advice, wasn't an unreasonable request, even though I knew it would cost me half an hour of my life that I was unlikely to get back. Whilst I have the utmost respect for her superior knowledge when it comes to the interpretation of plans, I did wonder if she might have been on the Strongbow again when she suggested that my new home was NOT a bungalow. As she became more and more exasperated by my failure to see what was clearly obvious to her, Jayne asked me to take another look at the external pictures of the house which, when I did, showed that the front elevation was a single storey building just as I had described it. Jayne further insisted that I turn my attention to the rear elevation, which clearly showed the ground floor windows and then several more above those. It transpired that the house was, in fact, a split level building, as I was now forced to admit. I had been so insistent on seeing what I wanted to be there that I had somehow managed to block out the reality of what actually was. Ultimately, this revelation did not dampen my enthusiasm for proceeding with the sale. My instincts told me that this was the right home for me at this stage in my life and, as most of my decisions are made trusting those inner feelings, I simply made a new promise to my knees that I would lose weight, made an offer of the full asking price (another bone of contention for Jayne) and flew off to play out in Florida the very next day. The following was written a month after I moved into my lovely home which I named the

Dolls House and in my eyes is still a bungalow, just with stairs.

28th November 2016

'Ooookay people… I have been here in the Dolls House for a month, a period of time which seems to have passed by in the blink of an eye. To say that the move, everything leading up to, and following it, was an epic negotiation would be a gross understatement of fact.

Kenny bless him, had extended our old home over the years to create lots of extra space which I had almost unconsciously set about filling with stuff. I was particularly efficient at filling any remaining void with my purchases of clothes and shoes during my first bout of cash incontinence. Of course I had given little, to no consideration of the size of the task awaiting me should the day come when I might need to relocate this vast collection into an area a third of the size, and my well-worn strategy of ignoring a problem until there is no choice but to deal with it, had not helped when the dawn of that day finally arrived. I knew that despite some charitable donations of items still complete with their price tags, including a yellow and black polka dot dress with matching shoes, which made me look like a giant cheese going mouldy from the bottom up, had not made much of an impact into the scale of the problem. I was shocked by the fact that in amongst the remaining items of clothes, there were no less than eight pairs of the same style of jeans, and identical dresses all purchased in multiples that I am too embarrassed to quantify. How can it be that a reasonably sane middle-aged woman well, middle-aged at least, can purchase the same items again and again without remembering having done so? Maybe my experimentation with alcohol in those days after losing Kenny has affected my cerebral functioning to a greater degree than I realised. Maybe the clothes mountain is symptomatic of actual brain damage, either way, I was overwhelmed by the undeniable evidence of my excesses, but not quite enough to stop me from buying another outfit to wear for the actual move.

The move itself was a feat of engineering, and my wonderful help at the time all had moments when they doubted the ability of my little Dolls House to absorb all the remaining contents of my former home, but as midnight approached the very last van load of items was finally forced into every available orifice.

In the month I have been here, my little house and I are slowly getting to know each other and the early signs are that we are going to get on just fine. I have tried to lessen the burden placed on the much smaller storage areas here by spending an inordinate amount of time at the local tip. To date, I have been invited by the guys who work there to their Christmas 'do' and told that I smelled nice too which, I took as a compliment until I remembered where I was. All in all, I am happy with my decision to move and where that decision has taken me. I am learning that I am capable of much more than I ever thought possible, though the need to be so, continues to be a great source of sadness in my life'.

Chapter 7

Dating sites and widows

The Guilt Monkey

As I have already talked about in the previous chapter, GOWNS, by the very nature of their membership to this particular group, learn to negotiate many old territories in new and different ways, but if there is one negotiation that stimulates greater debate over all the others, it is the prospect of another relationship. There are many hurdles that need to be cleared before reaching the point where you might start to contemplate what your life could be like if you were lucky enough to find a new partner to share it with. The inevitable feelings of guilt which accompany this consideration can create the most formidable of all those obstacles. GOWNS do guilt extremely well. We obsess about the fact that we survived when our partners did not, frequently revisiting their last days and hours to agonise over what we could, or should have done differently and, of course, we worry that we are not *good widows*, especially when we find our thoughts turn to the possibility of another relationship.

The anxiety can be crippling and, in my case, I found that by treating these emotions – that I knew were largely illogical – as an entity in their own right, I was better able to deal with them, so I blamed them on the antics of something I used to call the Guilt Monkey. I conjured up images of a mischievous primate who sat on my shoulder, where he tried to persuade me that the best way to avoid the feelings of guilt was to do absolutely nothing that might trigger them. He would encourage me to pour myself another drink and have a good old wallow and, when I took his advice, my anxiety levels did decrease. Then, of course, when the effects of the alcohol wore off, they would skyrocket out of control, further compounded by my self-loathing at my lack of self-regulation.

When the Guilt Monkey was successful in keeping my stress levels high and my positivity low, he was rewarded with a nice fat metaphorical banana but, by animating my inner thoughts in this way, I was gradually able to work out how to counter his arguments and, subsequently, starve him of his incentive to stay with me.

There were three things that Kenny asked me to do after he died and, at the time, I refused to openly acknowledge any of them, because I was still not prepared to admit that he would actually die. My refusal to acknowledge them did not mean that I hadn't heard his wishes and committed them to darkest recesses of my memory just in case. The first of these requests was that I should finish a novel I have written – he firmly believed that my interest in writing was going to be pivotal to my future survival without him. His second wish was that I should sell our home and go and enjoy a big new adventure and, thirdly, he wanted me to ensure that he remained a presence in the lives of the grandsons he adored. Later, as I sat pondering my late husband's requests, which typically were more about me than him, I did begin to contemplate finishing my novel, which initial interest agreed did have some commercial viability. Positivity of any kind, though, is tracked down faster than a biscuit barrel at a Weight Watchers meeting and, once alerted to it, the Guilt Monkey had soon parked his little pink arse back on my shoulder to begin his counter-intuitive attack. He agreed that my novel might indeed enjoy a level of success and, were I to sell the house, then I might be able to afford an adventure of the type that Kenny had wished for me. But, and this is the genius of the Guilt Monkey, by spending the family inheritance on a trip to Outer Mongolia to teach Morris dancing, would I then deprive my grandsons of the regular reminders of their granddad that he so wanted them to have? I could feel the presence on my shoulder excitedly anticipating the deliverance of another fistful of bananas until I asked him if he had ever heard of Skype. Clearly rattled by my new-found resistance to his influence, the Guilt Monkey pointed out my many deficits in the terms of modern technology, which was a fair point, albeit one made with scant regard of the more recent progress I had made in this area. If the tutorials on YouTube, I informed him, could show me how to milk a snake then it was a reasonable bet that I would be able to access all I needed to know about the workings of Skype too. Barring the odd resurgence of chatter as I continued to develop my technique of challenging him – something that I found was so much easier than having the same dialogue with myself – the Guilt Monkey eventually grew bored with my company and left to seek out a more receptive host with a larger supply of bananas.

This welcome departure opened up my thinking to lots of future possibilities, including something that, up until this point, had seemed abhorrent to me. Kenny had been a wonderful attentive husband and I missed him with every fibre of my being, but he was never coming back and I missed that feeling of being special to someone else, other than my grandchildren and my sister's dog. I missed sex too, which had been hugely important to both of us and the thought of remaining celibate and unloved in that way for the rest of my life was truly frightening to me.

Facing facts

As I took a long hard critical look at my fifty-year-old reflection, certain truths were inevitable. Long gone were the days when Kenny could encompass the circumference of my waist in a single hand, my chin looked like it had given birth to triplets, and my once dewy complexion had been replaced by something resembling the texture of an elephant's arse. If travelling to the south in winter is a destination of choice, then there were parts of me that had even beaten the Germans to the sunbeds. Just one of these features was a serious bar to success down the sausage aisle in Sainsbury's on singles night, but put them all together? Whilst I might have been able to count on the adoration of my late husband, even when the sight of my oversized grey knickers were all that greeted his romantic overtures, often accompanied by phrases such as *'remove your prick from my posterior, you inconsiderate prat'*, these were all behaviours that I knew would need to be seriously revised if I were to stand any chance of attracting a new romantic interest.

So, having made the decision to at least have a look around the terminal of travellers looking for future happiness with A.N. Other, I observed that this was a high traffic area with a populous as diverse as it was united in purpose. Some people identified with each other relatively quickly and happily made their way towards the departure gate to begin their respective journeys together. Those in this category were characterised by a seemingly endless supply of the energy synonymous with youth, a disregard for caution and a lustful appreciation of the beauty of the pre-middle aged form. Then there were those travellers who, for various reasons, were destined to have their travel plans marred by delays or cancellations. The pallor of age is pretty effective camouflage for an adventurous soul fighting for recognition underneath a sagging body that is no longer designed to attract the curious exploration of a loving partner.

The world has changed extensively in the forty or so years since I met, married and lost Kenny. The advent of social media and dating apps have revolutionised the way connections are made between members of the opposite sex, seeking relationships of potential depth or otherwise. As a businesswoman in my previous life, I understood the concept of marketing products effectively, and correct product placement is essential, as is the identification and promotion of a unique selling point. With this in mind, I decided to join an internet dating site for the over fifties which, in essence, is a lot like a charity shop window, full of second-hand goods looking for a good home.

I joined several dating sites because I suspected that the experiences of a widow negotiating the world of internet dating might be something that I would later write about and I was keen to learn to what extent that experience would differ, depending on the sites that I chose to use. The world of internet dating did reveal lots of surprises, but one that I had not expected was the way in which I became something of a target, surprisingly not from unscrupulous men hoping to exploit my perceived vulnerability, but from other bereaved spouses themselves. Apparently, whilst not judging me for wanting to explore the possibility of another relationship, I was told by some that due to the uniquely special relationships that they had enjoyed with their deceased partners, this would be an impossibility for them. There was also a percentage who said that, despite the death of their husband or wife, they still felt *married* and, therefore, any new relationship would feel adulterous and disloyal.

Given that we all grieve in our own individual ways, I do not doubt for a second that, these viewpoints, are completely valid and I respect them without question or judgement. However, having said that, am I then to agree that because I *was* able not only to consider a new relationship but to actively seek one out in whatever capacity suited me at the time, that my own relationship with Kenny was somehow less special than those who couldn't and didn't? Because it wasn't and I was deeply hurt by the implication. I also knew that my late husband would not have wanted me to limit my chances of future happiness by any misguided sense of loyalty to our marriage vows once he died, but if people were determined to view me as a *Merry Widow* there was little I could do to stop them. I can readily accept that some of my behaviours at the time may well have created the impression that losing my husband had opened up new avenues of enjoyment for me, but they were, in fact, symptomatic of the self-abuse I continued to inflict on myself in order to avoid dealing with the pain of what losing him actually meant.

'Never think that the length and breadth of your grief reflect the depth and breadth of your love.'

I discovered this quote on the *Dr Phil* show, which in itself might be enough for some to dismiss it as something less than profound, but to which I would add the following:

'I may not be grieving now in the way that I once was, but this is because I am learning to live alongside my own grief in my own way.'

That one came straight from the heart of a *Merry Widow* near you.

Safety on dating sites

Some of the practices that should help to preserve our safety when using dating sites seem, on the face of it, to be common sense and the following section includes good examples of precautions that everyone should take in order to keep themselves safe. Suffice to say that I ignored each and every one of them because, in reality, common sense can very easily be overridden by complacency and a false sense of your own impunity. Thankfully, and more by good luck than good judgement, I did not suffer any disastrous consequences as the result of my failure to adhere to much of any of the following, for which I remain eternally grateful.

Choose the right site

The world at large is an eclectic place and it goes without saying that there are sites out there that cater for a mind-boggling array of tastes, beliefs and lifestyle choices, so it is crucial that you choose carefully. If, for instance, I had a preference for a man sporting facial hair then there is a site which could have seen me running my fingers through an impressive array of beards in no time and, whilst my research did not unearth a site for those attracted to bearded ladies, it did unearth sites for people looking for no strings sex, larger lovers, fetishes and even salad eaters, so the importance of understanding the expectations of a site's membership cannot be overstated.

Free sites

There are many free dating sites to choose from out there but, because they require no monetary investment, this can mean that those using them might not be looking for serious, or for long term, relationships. This does not necessarily mean that paying to use the services of a dating site guarantees that those using it are any more inclined towards the pursuit of genuine relationships either, but it does at least imply some level of effort. The paid-for sites usually have the benefit of some degree of moderation too, though the effectiveness of this can vary significantly. Some sites allow you to join for free initially and this means that whilst you can complete a profile and add pictures – which gives you the opportunity to gauge any response – you are not allowed to communicate with anyone of interest until you decide to subscribe fully to the site. When you do decide to subscribe to a site that you feel fulfils your particular remit, then a number of other safety rules should come into play.

Stay on the site

It is inevitable that, at some point, that you will come across those whose intentions are far from honourable. Some of these are incredibly easy to spot, as in the time a picture of Paul Hollywood – he of *'Bake Off'* fame – popped up in my gallery, only now he was purporting to be Winston from Wales in an attempt to boost his appeal with the ladies? Then there are the far more sophisticated scammers out there too, who are not as easy to unmask. The golden rule is to stay on the site. Often, would-be scammers will encourage you to divulge your e-mail address or phone number, which they can then use for a variety of purposes. It should go without saying that you should never provide specific details of your surname or your address to anyone online at this stage.

Meeting up

When, and if, this stage is reached and an actual date is arranged, certain precautions are, as I have already said, just plain common sense. Never allow someone you don't know to pick you up from home. Arrange to meet in a busy public place and get someone to phone you after about half an hour to check that you are safe and to give you the opportunity to respond to some fake emergency if you feel the need to bail.

Google 'em!

Why not? You might find little to no information that will help you learn more about your potential date but, in a way, this could be a good thing if you believe that no news is good news. Someone I knew discovered that a man she planned to meet had several tattoos when she found his profile on Facebook, something he had gone to some lengths to hide in his pictures on the dating site. I did not agree with her conclusion that this meant he was some kind of arch-criminal, but it is never a good idea to lie in your profile or to post pictures of yourself that are misleading or benefit heavily from filters and other editing tools.

Food & drink

Usually, our expectations of a date are sufficiently high that, at the very least, we hope to make a good friend, if not a life partner but, though thankfully rare amongst internet daters in middle age, date rape can, and does happen. It makes sense to be vigilant concerning the whereabouts of your drink and any food to ensure that no noxious substances can be added.

Creating a profile

A profile is basically a form of advert through which you hope to *sell* yourself online and can be the difference between success and failure. I remember feeling like an awkward teenager as I experimented with my hair and makeup and then photographed the results, most of which I deleted for fear of traumatising my grandsons, should they find them on my phone. Given that my arms are about as long as an average Twiglet, the art of the selfie was a hard-earned skill but, with some effort and clever lighting, I was at last able to produce some pictures suitable for my profile, largely because they showed me from the neck up; anything below it was the subject of a work in progress about which I would worry later.

It's a bit embarrassing at my age to admit to being genuinely excited when I learned that someone had read my profile, looked at my pictures and decided that they would like to contact me. The site administrators are only too well aware of this and I learned that some of them are not above using fake profiles to encourage you to sign up to the site, after which these types of profiles tend to disappear. Such was the response to my profile, I remember thinking that I had severely underestimated the power of my matronly middle-aged allure, as row upon row of pixelated pictures kept appearing in my inbox and, for a while, I wasn't even able to have a conversation with the bloke in the local chip shop without assuming he fancied me, as least as much as he did a good portion of battered cod. Thankfully, the sepia mist around my rose-tinted spectacles soon cleared and I pulled the cloak of generational invisibility back over my inflated ego and reconnected with reality. The following is a profile I wrote for one of the sites that I was using.

My profile

'This is the bit where all the clichés fit I guess but I so don't want to do those. What I will say is that I have had a brilliant life so far and was lucky enough to be in a long happy marriage until I became widowed. I can

still smile and see the joy in people and places. I know who I am and have been accredited with having a BS radar which sorts out the pretenders in a Nanosecond, so integrity is key.

I am a natural optimist and my sense of humour is what has sustained me through all the good times I have been lucky to experience and, has kept me going through the times when my luck ran out. I love to be spontaneous and enjoy the unpredictable, whilst at other times I like to 'kickback' and be a spectator to the madness of others. I respond to kindness in like, love a good honest debate from the serious to the silly and all the stuff in between. I am looking for, and forward to, another great adventure...simples!!'

It's a good job that I was losing weight quite rapidly at this time, which made for better profile pictures because my written profile was ill-placed to win friends or influence people. Despite this, it wasn't long before my inbox began to fill up and one particular profile caught my eye. It was from a guy who lived in Manchester who was looking for a new long term relationship after losing his wife to cancer. His profile picture was far from unpleasant and depicted a suave looking middle-aged man, whose written profile appeared to be detailed and well written. I responded to his *wink*, a term which is dating speak for wanting to strike up a conversation and awaited the following reply.

'Hello Sandra

My name is Johns, I am very good honest mans, and I like to spoil my beautiful lady and treat her like the princess she was born to be. I really like your smiles, and I want to rescue you from your tower by climbing up your hair and taking you to a house of bliss, where you would be happy every day and free from your pains

Love from Johns.'

It is easily apparent to anyone with even the loosest command of English that the guy who wrote the above was not a native of Manchester and his profile information seemed to have been written by someone else entirely. Also, as I had definitely not mentioned my arthritic knees in my own profile information, I wondered just what type of pain it was that might be improved by a visit to a *'house of bliss'*. If I had fully expected to receive approaches from scammers, I was a little deflated to have experienced this so early into my foray, nevertheless, I decided to play along with Johns for a little while longer and sent him the following

'Dear Johns

How very lovely to meet you both. Thank you for your messages especially as like me you have experienced grief and loss in your life. How long is it since you were widowed?

Sandra'.

The response, when it came, saw me laughing out loud with an abandonment I had not known since Kenny died.

'Hello again princess Sandra

You make me very happy mans in my life, I wish you happy and yes please, I want to be widows just like you.

Love from Davids'.

It was obvious to me that Johns/Davids had a split personality disorder and that I had been introduced to both of them. In truth, a lot of scams originate from countries such as Nigeria and people are often contacted by several men purporting to be the same person. They tend to work in shifts and, in this case, they had simply neglected to sustain continuity in respect of who they were claiming to be. If I considered myself to be a fairly savvy operator who thought she understood her own vulnerability (looking back at the risks I took I was actually clueless), I was surprised by the fact that even knowing that this was a clear attempt at deception, probably for financial gain, quite bizarrely, a part of me really still hoped that it wasn't.

The following message is another example of a scammer that is easily identifiable, and again his use of English provides the biggest clue.

'Sandra

I enjoy your illustrations, you have big smile and big teeth. If you mind we can meet I want to put my hands on your beautiful head hair.

From Benjamin Sargent'.

Beginning to despair of finding any messages in my inbox that didn't sound like they had been written in a hut in the Congo, I dutifully penned my response.

'Dear Benjamin

How very kind of you to send me a compliment on my hair, by the way, you are not related to Goldie Hawn are you by any chance? My 'hair' is actually a wig I wear at weekends, and on special occasions when I stop being bald old Sidney and become sultry Sandra instead. Thank you for boosting my confidence as I am now thinking that I should become Sandra full time.

From Sid'.

Not expecting a reply, I was surprised to see one which congratulated me on my dual citizenship and asked if I could send him some money for a phone card so that we could talk in person. I declined on this occasion, though I did agree to speak to a much more sophisticated scammer on the phone later on, in order to fully understand the methods that these highly organised groups use to exploit vulnerable women on dating sites.

Gradually I began to form the following categories which seemed to me to sum up the main reasons that men were frequenting the sites I visited.

The scammers

In light of the aforementioned, this category is somewhat self-explanatory, though we should include in this group men who fail to disclose that they are married and are, in fact, only looking for some extracurricular activity on the side.

The barely breathers

This category consisted of very elderly men whose demise was likely imminent or, if their profile pictures were anything to go by, might well have already happened. Generally, the men in this group were seeking the company of females willing to participate in a carer with *benefits* type of arrangement. I was asked by one game old geezer if I had any objection to him eating fried eggs directly from my naked breasts. I replied, only if he liked ostrich eggs as your regular hen sized job was unlikely to provide the required coverage, before blocking any further messages from him. Not all the messages I received from men in this group were of this ilk, and I did get some lovely messages from those who were lonely and just happy to have the opportunity to chat with a woman for a while. When I complained to Fred (not his real name) who was eighty-one, that despite using both a map and a compass I was beginning to despair of ever finding a remotely suitable date, let alone a real relationship prospect, he sent me the following message in response.

'No darling maps and compasses are of no use to you on this site. What you would find useful though is a good prat nav because anyone who cannot see the kind soul lurking behind that beautiful face of yours deserves to show up on your screen so you can steer well clear of them. Take very good care of yourself and stay safe

The perverts

Although there are some of these in the above category, here I am referring to the more sinister type that deserves a classification all of their own. Initially, they might be quite difficult to spot because their early messages are usually quite inoffensive and generally charming, which usually extends throughout the duration of messages exchanged on the site, though not always. I did have one experience where a man wrote me a message worthy of inclusion in the pages of any highly pornographic publication, just past the stage of hello. The problem with this group is that it is easy to promote them into my next category which contains the profiles of the *ifs, buts & maybes*. Once they have achieved their reclassification, though, usually along with your phone number, this is often the point at which their communications begin to adopt a more sexually graphic tone and photographs of appendages in various stages of excitement start to take up space in your phone's photo gallery. At one stage, I had a collection of phallic examples ranging from everything the size of a glue stick to those the size of a foot-long sub. Even though I clearly understood the agenda of these individuals, in that these were not men looking for anything other than sex, either over the phone or in person, I was shocked by the extent to which I was prepared to engage with them, irrespective of how far short of the mark they fell in terms of what I was looking for myself

The ifs, buts & maybes

By far the smallest of all the categories, which contained the profiles of men I considered to be at least worthy of investigation, and resulted in a variety of different experiences and outcomes.

The serial winkers

As previously alluded to, winking on a dating site is a way of showing someone that you are interested. Exponents of this mechanism argue that it is easier than sending a message to someone who has no interest in responding to it, so basically saving them time and effort.

This was quite an interesting group in that its members seemed to be decent enough guys who didn't show any of the tendencies or behaviours required to gain admission to any of the other categories and, but for their serial winking, might even have made it into the 'ifs, buts & maybes' collective. One of the sites I frequented allowed you to keep a *dating diary* to which I was a regular contributor. The following is one such diary entry written about the serial winker:

'Ooookay people...I do not like the term winking, for me, it has a very Lesley Philips 'ding dong' type of connotation to it which seems a little strange in the context of its use on a dating site aimed at those of us of a more mature vintage. Whilst I understand that the act of winking has an immediacy about it, it is the act of winking habitually that remains a mystery to me. Often winkers will do so several times each day, on most days of the week which when you add it up over the period of a month, amounts to a seriously exhausting amount of winking. On the occasions that I have tried to respond to this type of winker with a message, I am usually ignored though they continue to wink away at a furious pace whilst steadfastly refusing to engage beyond this. I have no option but to assume that maybe winkers like this are so sufficiently satisfied by the act of winking alone, that they have no actual need to proceed further than a wink do you think?'

My first internet date

The very first date that I went on or, perhaps more accurately, didn't go on will be forever etched into my memory. I had been conversing online with a chap for some weeks though, if I am honest, there was nothing particularly interesting about him except that he didn't sound like he deserved to be included in one of the more sinister of my categories, probably not even the *ifs, buts & maybes* either. By now, though, I was becoming desperate to experience an actual date and

I agreed to meet him at a garden centre central to both our locations, despite my reservations.

In his profile Andrew (not his real name) had described himself as six feet tall and, from his photographs, seemed to be of average looks and listed his interests to be designer clothes, fine dining, travel and the theatre. My choice of clothes has never been made on the basis of their label, but I reasoned that I scrubbed up reasonably well regardless, and I liked food too, even if my tastes were more Gastro pub than Michelin starred. I loved to travel and enjoyed the theatre on occasion, so surely this should be enough to sustain a conversation for a while at least, I reasoned. The day of the date arrived and the weather was fabulous, forcing the mercury up into the low eighties. I tried to be excited and dressed to impress but my instincts were telling me that I should not get my hopes up, so I decided that I would approach it much as I would a business meeting. I set off early, as I absolutely hate being late for anything, even the things I don't really want to do, and arrived at the Garden Centre with half an hour to spare. Sitting in a car on a hot summer's day was not helpful to the integrity of my eyeliner, so I decided that I would lurk outside the display of garden sheds, opposite the café where Andrew and I had arranged to meet.

The time of our liaison drew closer and, from my vantage point at the top of a long walkway, I spotted an image, not unlike those I had viewed online, only with one or two vital differences. The person walking towards me seemed to have left at least two feet of his pre-described six-foot frame at home, making him even shorter than me at five feet nothing in socks, only today I was wearing heels that elevated me by another four inches or so. On top of this, I noticed that, for a man with a keenly developed sense of fashion, the choice of what seemed to be an outfit not unlike a striped pair of pyjamas, and un-ironed ones at that, seemed an odd choice of attire for a first date.

For reasons that I do not fully understand to this day, I found myself opening the door of one of the display sheds and closing it quickly behind me. I pleaded with my arthritic knees to allow me to take up a crouching position inside the wooden structure, which had already assumed the persona of a Swedish sauna, before daring to peep through the shed window, to see Andrew arrive at the café as planned. Then, on hearing voices approaching my shed, I was forced to hold onto the door with all the tenacity of a terrier with a ferret in its jaws, which thankfully proved to be enough to persuade the inquisitors outside to assume that the shed was locked but, by now, Andrew was making determined strides directly towards my hiding place. Realising too late that my phone was not on silent when his number flashed up on the caller display, I fought like a woman deranged to turn it off with one hand, whilst maintaining my vice-like grip of the door with the other. This was a position I was forced to maintain for a further twenty minutes before Andrew finally realised that he had been stood up and began to proceed back down the walkway towards the exit of the garden centre.

Once I could be sure that it was safe to do so, I emerged from the now blistering confines of the shed, gasping for air and leaking like a triangular teabag. My carefully coiffed curls dripped limply around what was left of my melted foundation and eyeliner and, when I tried to walk, my soaking wet feet squelched around in my stiletto heels, making noises not dissimilar to that of several rapid farts, as I made my way back to my car.

I was deeply shocked by my behaviour and struggled for ages to understand it. I am a confident outgoing person who enjoys meeting new people and, even though I had quickly deduced that Andrew and I were an unlikely match, this did not excuse my sudden decision to avoid meeting him once I had promised that I would. My attempts at an apology fell on deaf ears and, understandably, I never heard from him again, though I still wonder if internet dating was successful for him in the end.

My first date did not turn out to be my last by far and I did go on to meet quite a few men during my two years of what I loosely like to call my period of research on behalf of GOWNS contemplating the use of dating sites. Some of them remain good friends to this day; some were, uncharacteristically for me, nothing more than one night stands. At least once I convinced myself that I had fallen in love and committed bigamy when I got *married* in Vegas. I dated a boxer and a pot-smoking Scotsman who was fifteen years my junior and with whom I spent our first date at the funeral of my best friend. I have written accounts of all of these and other encounters in my next book *'The Funny Thing About Being a Widow – on a Dating Site'*.

Chapter 8

Time to face the music

Secondary drowning

I was sitting in my office in the Dolls House, watching the world go by, or at least as much of it as you can observe when living in a cul-de-sac, trying hard to ignore the blank expanses of A4 staring out at me from the screen on my laptop, when my meanderings turned to Lisa. When Kenny became ill the demands of a large five bedroomed house, along with the increase in his care needs and chasing a miracle cure, all began to take their toll, so I decided to find someone to help me with the housework. Lisa turned out to be an absolute Godsend. Not only was she thoroughly efficient at her job and completely trustworthy, but her sunny personality was something I looked forward to encountering each week. When Kenny died I asked Lisa if she would stay on; if the constraints on my time had lessened considerably, then so had any inclination to do my own cleaning and, quite apart from this, I was by now more dependent on the poor girl than was probably healthy.

This became clearly apparent during the morning I awoke to find a body of water the size of a small lake in my living room. I was completely clueless as to what steps to take to deal with this crisis, apart from wish with all my heart that Kenny was still around to send me out to shop for shoes. I realised that this was a time to think on my feet which, were already submerged up to my ankles, so I promptly ordered a canoe from Amazon prime, then phoned Lisa to ask her what to do until it was delivered. Given that I have never stopped a cock in my life and had no idea what I was supposed to be looking for, or even where to look for it, my sense of relief when Lisa arrived and took charge of dealing with my unwelcome indoor water feature was total. In no time she had secured the services of a local plumber to fix my leaking toilet, the apparent cause of the problem, promptly dealt with my house insurers, which meant that I got to spend a pleasant afternoon picking out a nice new carpet, before finally cancelling the canoe.

Whilst I was grateful that Lisa had restored calm from out of the chaos, I was also angry with myself and the depths of my ineptitude, which had undoubtedly been caused in no small way by Kenny's tendency to treat me as though I were disabled, not because *he* considered me to be inept in any way but because his inclination had always been to protect me from worrying about anything if he could deal with it first.

Lisa did move with me to the *Dolls House* but, inevitably, as the demands of her young family grew less, she was always deservedly destined for pastures new.

I resigned myself to the fact that my housework sabbatical was over, because I didn't want someone else in my home who wasn't Lisa and, whilst I managed to keep on top of things initially without her, the *Dolls House* slowly began to show signs of neglect as the result of my declining interest. This was especially evident in my office, which was in dire need of some re-organisation, but the mess just gave me another welcome excuse to avoid going in there to start work.

 I noticed that the level of activity in the cul-de-sac this morning was even less than usual, now that the regular dog walkers, who used to allow their canines to crap on my drive, had started actually using the pooh bags they kept hidden in their pockets to use in more densely populated areas, where they would then be whipped out with all the aplomb of a magician pulling a rabbit out of a hat, after which they would animatedly proceed to clean up after their dogs as though this had always been their intention.

This change in behaviour had been prompted after I started to lurk surreptitiously behind the partially closed blinds in my office, which allow me to see out but prevented people from seeing in. I would then sit in wait of a serial offender and, just at the point I could be sure that the crap was not going home in either the dog or a pooh bag, I would quickly open the blinds to reveal my presence. If this proved to be an effective way of ensuring that my drive remained turd free, the same might not have been true of the undergarments worn by the dog's owner when alerted to my unexpected presence. The downside to this decrease in activity outside was that it left me even more time to spend staring at white space on my laptop and, increasingly desperate to avoid this particular agony, I reluctantly turned my attention to my surroundings and conceded that something really should be done to improve them.

There were a whole jumble of files that should have been neatly stored in cabinets specifically designed for this purpose but were strewn all over the spare bed in my office instead. This meant that they were now proving to be a significant barrier between me and the duvet which I, all too readily, tended to slip under when I had exhausted all of my usual excuses to eschew sitting at my desk. The dust, at least, was sufficiently thick to be utilized as auxiliary shelving but, on this particular morning, I decided that the time had come to try to restore some semblance of order to my workspace. I also hoped that, by effecting such a re-organisation, it might help to encourage my creative juices back to full flow, given that they had been reduced to a mere trickle of late.

I pulled on a pair of bright yellow Marigolds and some shiny surfaces started to re-emerge as I wiped away the layers of dust but, predictably, it wasn't long before I was contemplating the quickest route through the files on the bed towards the underside of the duvet. The rubber gloves had made my hands sweat profusely and, as I peeled them off, I became suddenly inspired to adapt them towards a different use entirely. Quite how I managed to stay conscious through the not inconsiderable effort it took to blow one of them up enough so that I could stick it on my head and pretend to a cockerel was nothing short of a miracle. I squawked and flapped my imaginary wings until, and much later than I would have liked, I became aware that one of the regular dog walkers was watching my performance through blinds that I had inadvertently forgotten were still open after a previous *reveal*. This particular chap was sporting the kind of grin that you might not normally expect to see on the face of someone scraping up shit. Gleefully, he waved his fully utilised pooh bag in the direction of my office window and I smiled through gritted teeth by way of a response before telling him to go *'cluck himself'*, or something very similar.

The point here is that, whilst outwardly I appeared to be functioning well enough, at least when I wasn't wearing a rubber glove attached to my head, the truth was that I wasn't coping anywhere near as well as I tried to make it appear. Now that I had negotiated most of the things that I would ever have to do alone for the first time, and all that remained was the prospect of repeating this process, again and again, was enough to send me into a deep state of inertia.

After speaking with lots of GOWNS over the years, I learned that my dread of those *'Second Firsts'*, that Christina Rasmussen talks about in her aforementioned book of the same name, was, by no means, unique to me. Sometimes this stage is regarded as being just as painful as the raw cloying grief we experience during the early days after our loss. If the onset of grief has a clearly discernible starting point which, in my case, was when Kenny received his diagnosis of gastric cancer, then the same is not true in terms of a clearly defined finishing line, because grief doesn't end and we don't come out of it at the other side, in the way people like to imagine. Neither is it a process which follows an ascending trajectory but is more likely to be characterised by majorly high moments which are then followed by those the exact opposite, just as I was now beginning to properly understand for myself.

When Kenny died, my circumstances were such that I had no choice but to carry on working. At the time I regarded this to be probably a good thing in that it deprived me of the opportunity to wallow and kept my attention focused on keeping a number of balls in the air. Looking back now, I can see how working hard was just another mechanism that I used, in the same way, that I had used alcohol and men, as a way of shutting out the pain of losing my husband.

My intention was to keep on working until I managed to save up enough money to support myself during a year off so that I could finish writing this book and work on several other projects which are also very dear to my heart. When I did eventually finish work, if I thought that this would bring me a step closer to the realisation of my ambitions, then I couldn't have been more wrong.

Instead of beating a pathway towards the door of my office, brimming with ideas and excited by the new freedoms that came with my newly unemployed status, inexplicably, I went from being a confirmed insomniac to being unable to get out of bed in the morning. Even at the height of my drinking, I managed to stay functional and punctual, if perhaps to a slightly lesser degree than I imagined at the time, but, by now, I was hardly functioning at all. To add insult to injury, an old adversary made an unwelcome return in the form of the Guilt Monkey, who was quick to take full advantage of my state of self-doubt and diminishing confidence. His chatter was incessant as he tried to persuade me that it was absolutely fine to leave those sheets of A4 in their persistently unblemished state. He qualified this further with a quote from Mother Theresa, who had apparently once said that in order to finish anything you had to start it first. The Guilt Monkey's argument was simple: if I didn't start writing in the first place, then I had no need to worry about finishing it either. The more persuasive part of his argument drove straight at the heart of my fear of being held up to scrutiny and I decided that I should probably abandon my writing ambitions and go and get myself a job cleaning toilets instead.

My descent into the depths continued apace with my concentration span consistently refusing to extend beyond that of a particularly stupid Goldfish, and the step counter app on my phone assumed that I had died when, after several days, there was no activity registered to prove that I hadn't. The physical effects of this *secondary drowning* were becoming increasingly obvious too: although my interest in all things culinary had never quite reached the heights I enjoyed whilst Kenny was alive, I did recover enough of an interest to make reasonably good choices in terms of what I was eating. At this point, all my dietary needs were pretty much being met by deliveries from Domino's Pizza and I started to gain weight in increments of a stone at a time, rather than a pound here and there. I was grateful, though, that my consumption of alcohol miraculously did remain under control so, at least, I was fully aware of what was happening to me, even if I was still powerless to stop it.

At one stage I started a food diary, so that I could monitor what I was eating, the hope being that a visual record of my excesses might shock me into to reducing them. Looking on the bright side, I was at least writing again, but then there are only so many times you can pen the word pizza on an otherwise empty page, so I gave up the food diary on the day I realised that I had been inadvertently trying to eat its cover. My long lazy days were sometimes punctuated by the odd flurry of activity and I even got as far as setting up my music keyboard beside the one on my laptop in the office. I learned to play the piano as a child and I hoped that, if I started to play music again, it might re-ignite some kind of interest in a life that was by now passing me by at a rate of knots.

It had been my father who encouraged me to take up the piano; he didn't play himself but both of his elder brothers were able to play any piece after hearing it just once. When I showed a flicker of some ability, my father was determined that I should learn to play and read music, so he sent me for private lessons. My tutor was a lady called Esme, a nasty old harridan who had a tendency to rap my knuckles when I hit a wrong note, or when she considered my timing to be off. In the end and thoroughly fed up with this treatment, I took to hiding around the corner from Esme's house for the duration of the half an hour lesson, after which I returned home as usual. Of course, this solution was never destined to be more than a temporary one and when my father found out the reason for my sudden disinterest he hit the roof. After a visit from him, during which he suggested several other uses for Esme's ruler, which it's possible that as a spinster she might not have fully understood, she was soon replaced by a weasel-faced little man called Ronnie.

By now my father had invested in a Hammond organ, no doubt hoping that this might encourage me towards becoming the female version of Reginald Dixon, who used to rise up on his mighty Wurlitzer at weekends in the Tower Ballroom at Blackpool. Unfortunately, Ronnie's hands were seldom where they were paid to be during our lessons and, fearing that his fate would be far worse than that of Esme after a few lessons I simply told my father that I was confident that, now I had mastered the basics, I could probably improve by practice alone. I did manage to reach to a passable, if unremarkable, standard and my credits included playing badly in a band, a clutch of appearances in local pubs and clubs and being compared to Mrs Mills a couple of times, but only on account of our similar build, not our playing ability. At the time of writing this, I have yet to turn on my Technics SX-KN6000 keyboard, let alone attempt to play it.

Swimming back to the surface

The bottom of anything is not usually thought of as being a good place. Whether it means finishing in the bottom half of a race, languishing on the bottom rung of a ladder or even the way in which most of us consider that our own bottoms are not exactly things of beauty, either because they are too fat, the wrong shape or especially when we think that someone is using theirs for the purposes of speech. I, on the other hand, have some respect for this much-maligned and lowly position. The truth is that when we do reach the bottom of anything this is when some of the old clichés rightly persist, largely because they often contain a grain of truth. For instance, how many times do we tell ourselves *the only way is up* when a period of freefall comes to an end because the bottom line has finally been reached? I was ecstatic when the moment arrived when my not inconsiderable arse connected fully with my own rock bottom because I knew that it was time, at last, for me to swim back to the surface and to resume my life in whatever ways fate would decree that I should. There were a number of things that helped me to regain perspective on my situation and it was two of the dearest friends I ever had who helped me to send the Guilt Monkey on his way once and for all.

Pauline

'It has been said that a party without a cake is quite simply a meeting. Well, if this is true then my fabulous friend Pauline was not only the cake that could change any meeting into a party, but she was also the icing on the top of it too. Some thirty or more years ago good fortune would dictate that our paths should cross and, once they had, I was immediately attracted to Pauline's spirit and energy, much like a moth is attracted to a flame. As I learned later, Pauline was actually quite a shy person, who often spoke to me about her lack of confidence. I hope I was able to reassure her that this was not something that was obvious to anyone on meeting her. She was warm, engaging and able to put people at ease within moments – even now, as I recall this simple truth about my dearest friend, I am smiling.

Pauline was, in today's vernacular, a lunchtime organiser or, in the parlance of those of us over a certain age, a dinner lady, though to the children my friend was simply known as Aunty Pauline. Political correctness had no relevant place in her world: if a child tripped and scraped a knee, or felt sick at the prospect of being made to eat spotted dick, semolina or, worse still, sago pudding and prunes, then it was Pauline who would ensure that this was the child who got a comforting hug, a tissue or a pass to the back of the dinner queue, where supplies of the offending desserts always seemed to run out just before it was their turn.

There are a lifetime of shared memories between my buddy and me, and I have struggled to choose those which best illustrate her many fine qualities. Family was at the core of her being and as a mum, grandma, aunty or friend she was largely unrivalled in terms of her unconditional love for them all. However, as I have sat over the last few days with her children John and Emma and we have reminisced and laughed about the wonderful legacy of happiness she has left behind, I was also struck by the different ways in which the memories we all made together are recalled so differently by the younger generation. For instance, one of the things that Pauline and I shared was our love of music. She had an almost photographic memory for song lyrics, which was not restricted in any way by genre or date, and I thought that she had a rather lovely singing voice too, which certainly added much to my inferior keyboard skills. In the days before The X-Factor, we would delude ourselves that we might have scored well on Hughie Green's opportunistic clapometer and, on each Christmas Eve, Pauline and I would gather the children around the keyboard to sing carols, pleased that we were doing our bit to support a tradition which, even back then, was evolving into something much less understandable to both of us. However, when talking with John and Emma, their recollections were not of warm Christmas jumpers, mulled wine and families viewed in soft focus through frost-framed windows. Apparently, their own recollections are more closely associated with bleeding eardrums and wishing that the wands they found in their boxes of magic tricks on Christmas morning really did have the power to put a stop to mine and Pauline's musical contributions.

Our families shared many wonderful holidays in Florida. Pauline and I spent many an hour within the pleasant confines of the Budweiser beer school, hoping to further our education. At the last count, I think we had achieved twenty-seven graduation certificates each which is a reflection of the serious way in which we applied ourselves to our extensive research at the complimentary bar.

 However, our enthusiasm and literal thirst for knowledge resulted in Pauline and me learning a different, though no less valuable, type of lesson too. At first, the brake lights ahead of us, as we drove back to the villa, proved to be of no particular concern, but the happy beer-infused banter was soon replaced by the kind of concerned silence caused by our now seriously challenged bladders which, in the case of middle-aged ladies wearing shorts, takes this concern to a whole new level. Suffice to say that a 7/11 store *was eventually located, just in time to save one of us, at least, some huge embarrassment. I have never been more grateful, as the navigator on those trips, for my front seat position in the van, as it gave me a head start towards the only available toilet. Sorry, Pauline, I should have, at the very least, offered to wash your shorts.*

Well, my fabulous, funny friend all that remains for me to say to you is thank you – thank you for your constant and consistent support over more years than I care to remember. Thank you for the many, many laughs we enjoyed together and which will live forever in my heart and help me to stem the sadness at your passing, with thoughts of how amazingly lucky I was to have you as my friend. Thank you too for teaching me the meaning of true friendship. God bless, Pauline, say hello to a certain cheeky chappie you might run into at Heaven's bar tonight and have one for me'.

Pauline died from COPD on 16th March 2016 as I, along with her beloved son and daughter, held her by the hand. The above was the tribute that I wrote to read at her funeral and, hopefully, needs nothing further added to it to convince anyone of just how hugely important she was and how much of an impact losing her had on me, especially coming as it did so soon after losing Kenny.

Catherine

I met Catherine when I moved on from selling my skills as a hairdresser to importing hair care products sourced from America instead and Catherine was employed by the sales arm of our distribution company. Bless her, she was everything that I am not – she was a statuesque Amazonian figure and, with me being a mere five feet tall in my stocking feet, this meant that I spent an inordinate length of time conversing with her breasts and avoiding her enthusiastic hugs, for fear of suffocation. Catherine had a zest for life that was truly infectious and, one time, she was genuinely thrilled when I taught her some ballet steps in the front room of her tiny Cambridgeshire cottage, which I told her came from a special production that had been written just for me called the *sugar plump fairy.* She thought that this was absolutely amazing: for a highly intelligent girl, there was no doubting that Catherine had her gullible moments. She used to say that I was the North to her South because she liked my tendency to call a spade a spade and, for myself, I never tired of introducing my sophisticated friend to others as a soft shandy swilling southern bastard.

Catherine was your archetypal posh bird and spoke accordingly and, I remember once when we were in a pub frequented by the local farmers near my rural home, the strikingly beautiful Catherine soon held them all in rapture, especially when they learned that she was far more down to earth than her demeanour suggested. After a few pints had been pulled and drank, the subject turned to the North/South divide, and the ruddy-faced farmers were soon boasting of their superior prowess when it came to their ability to work their way across the contents of the top shelf. Not one to shy away from a challenge, Catherine gamely took up the gauntlet and proceeded to put down each of the drinks offered to her until she had drawn level with the farmers. Only one drink remained untouched on the top shelf and even the hardiest of them flatly refused to take it on, so they put a hundred pounds on top of the bar, telling Catherine that it was hers for the taking, if she did. Without flinching, or even asking what was in the drink, she told them to put another fifty quid on top and they had got themselves a bet, which they did willingly. Feeling that the farmers looked far too confident that their money was safe, I began to worry that Catherine might live to regret risking her southern pride on this particular wager. The drink was poured and, sure enough, Catherine knocked it back in the same way as she had all the others whilst the farmers began to nudge and wink at each other, as though waiting for something. Catherine continued to stand impassively at the bar and their expressions became increasingly incredulous and, apparently completely unaffected by the potency of this drink, my friend casually scooped up her winnings, leaving the hard-drinking reputation of my fellow Northerner's in tatters and their pockets empty. Then she asked me to accompany her to the ladies room to help her with a, particularly awkward zip. Once we were safely behind closed doors Catherine started to retch uncontrollably causing liquid to pour out of every orifice, as it transpired that the drink she had so blithely consumed had been infused with one of the most potent chillies ever grown. Acting quickly and, even though she was convinced that her head was burning like a bonfire on Burns Night, Catherine mopped her face, quickly re-applied her makeup, and strode back into the bar, looking as elegant and as unfazed as ever. The story of the hard-core southern bird who had defeated the farmers on their top-shelf challenge became the stuff of local legend and, as far as I know, Catherine remains the only one to have ever won it.

My beautiful friend died in her local hospice on the 16th March 2016 from metastatic cancer, whilst I was holding Pauline's hand on the same day in another. Because Catherine had been aware of the fact that her cancer was terminal and incurable, she planned her own funeral down to the finest detail.

Her family and friends all gathered at a local woodland outside of Plymouth, where Catherine had settled in her latter years, and I gasped when I caught sight of her coffin, which was covered with pictures of thousands of bluebells taken against the backdrop of a dazzlingly blue sky which she, as a keen photographer, had taken herself. After we followed her down to a clearing in the woodland, we took our seats on tree stumps and listened to one of her friends tell us that Catherine requested that there should be no tears today, unless they were those caused by laughter. Of course, for most of us, this was easier said than done and the mood remained a sombre one until a cockerel made his presence known by crowing loudly and repeatedly, the timing of which caused a ripple of laughter to grow into that of helpless laughter. Later, at the crematorium, the curtains around Catherine's coffin closed gently to the fading strains of The Carpenters, bringing the proceedings to a close but, just as people began to leave, suddenly the curtains re-opened and the music started again, causing the kind of uncontrollable giggling that Catherine had insisted should mark this occasion. I fervently believe that she made her presence felt at her own funeral to ensure that her instructions were carried out to the letter.

Black hat guy

'The best things in life come when you least expect them' —this is undoubtedly a glib and unreliable yardstick but then I think of the woman who has all but given up on having a family of her own, only to realise that same ambition once she has let go of any hope of ever doing so. How often do we find ourselves saying that we have been pleasantly surprised by something we never expected would happen? And, yes, I totally accept that not all unexpected surprises are good ones, as GOWNS know only too well.

Barely surveying the usual array of the good, the bad and the downright ugly, which swam from right to left at the bottom of my screen on an internet dating site, my eye was drawn briefly towards the picture of a guy who was wearing a large black hat. This obscured his features slightly and, for lots of reasons, none of them good, some guys won't post a profile picture of themselves (a practice they are highly critical of when it comes to a woman who does the same), electing instead to replace them with pictures of their cat, for instance, or a large fish they claim to have caught, or, as on one occasion, when I was winked at by a guy who appeared to be a supermarket trolley. I am not sure why, but I didn't get the sense that this guy was deliberately trying to hide under his hat, so I hovered over his picture and decided to send him a message which contained just four words: *'I want that hat'*. As I pressed send, I was momentarily reminded of Kenny's extensive collection of hats, a lot of which I had given away before my move to the *Dolls House*, keeping just a few of his favourites. Looking again at black hat guy, I thought how ironic it would be if something were to develop between him and myself, given that it would have been a hat that prompted our first communication, though I wasn't really even expecting a coherent reply to my message, let alone much else.

The reply, when it came, explained that the hat wasn't actually owned by the guy wearing it – the picture had been taken when he tried it on for a laugh in a charity shop and he added that, if it were possible, he would gladly have given it to me. I scrutinised the message, as I always did when looking for obvious clues which might alert me to the agenda of any guy, but the spelling and punctuation of black hat guy, indicated that English was more than likely to be his first language and even seemed to suggest that he had been educated to a level that went beyond the mere Neanderthal. To be fair, there were a couple of other guys of whom this was also true but, generally speaking, finding anyone who could string a reasonable sentence together was sufficiently rare to at least heighten my curiosity.

I have chosen to talk about Pauline and Catherine here, not just because they were the most amazing and supportive friends in life, but, as I recall the agony of losing them both on the same day, I like to think that this might have been as the result of some collaboration on their part to remind me that, despite everything, I still have the one thing that both they and Kenny were denied and that is the luxury of time. I look at Pauline's beautiful grandchildren and know how much pleasure and pride she would have felt in watching them grow up and Catherine, who still had so much potential to exploit, that will now never be realised because her time was cruelly cut short. I can hear them both telling me that it is high time for me to get my head out of my arse, stop feeling sorry for myself and get on with my life before time runs out for me too. Message received and understood, girls, thank you.

Black hat guy is also mentioned in the context of my rescue from secondary drowning, because he also played a pivotal part in leading me back towards the surface, although there were many more signs for me to read in this respect as to what role, if any, a man with a big black hat might have to play in my future.

Chapter 9

Signs of the future

Till death us do part?

A lot has happened during the last four years or so, and there have been many changes in my life during this time, but the one thing that remains constant is the feeling that Kenny is still very much a part of my life. Maybe it's because we knew each so well that I instinctively hear his voice in answer to the questions I ask myself but, at times, his continuing influence appears to extend beyond the scope of this particular explanation of it. Not that I spend my days watching out for signs of his approval or otherwise, in respect of my solo decisions, but sometimes I can sense his presence very keenly. This chapter contains many examples of how this manifests itself but, on one evening, when I still lived in my old house and was engaged in a telephone conversation, I became distracted by what looked like little orbs of pale green light about the size of ten pence pieces dancing around my feet. The flooring in the old house was sparkly black granite and, as usual, I was wearing a fair amount of bling, so I assumed that what I was seeing was a trick of the light, though the orbs continued to float around the room for a few moments after I put the phone down. Later, in bed, I was wide awake as usual after a minimal amount of sleep but that night, for some reason, I was exceptionally restless and agitated. My bedroom was on the second floor and, once I climbed the two flights of stairs leading up to them, I never, ever went back down them again until morning. Unable to shrug off a growing sense of unease, I reluctantly decided on this occasion to venture back downstairs. As I opened the kitchen door, it felt unusually warm, especially as there hadn't been any heating on and, as I got nearer to the range cooker, it soon became clear why this was. I had left two of the electric hotplates on and hanging directly above them was a tea towel, that was just starting to smoulder, and was only moments away from igniting completely.

I was very shaken up by the thought of what might have happened but for my timely intervention, when I recalled those little orbs of floating light and I was curious to see if I could replicate the effects I had seen earlier. Even when I waved all my diamante at various angles under the spotlights, I was only able to produce the odd glint that reflected sharply off the granite floor, which was very different from what I had seen.

Later in the day I did some research and came across some photographs, which appeared to show small orbs of light that did seem to be very similar in size and shape to those I had witnessed earlier, and were described as being *'spheres of energy from the spiritual realm,'* which is an explanation you are either predisposed to believe or not. As I have cited in an earlier chapter, religion has no role to play in my life and it is, of course, possible that my fortuitous discovery was down to another coincidence, but the simple facts are that I did see orbs of light, whatever their origin, and because of my decision to go back downstairs, when I would never have normally done so, I was able to prevent a potentially life-threatening fire from developing.

Being my own worst enemy

After our initial exchange of messages, the black hat guy, who I had by now taken to calling the BHG, agreed to meet up for dinner, though at the time I was still flirting with the idea that a previous on-off relationship might be resurrected, even though in my heart I knew that not only that it couldn't, but shouldn't. The BHG was new to internet dating and my message had been the first that he had received, and when I met him I was not disappointed. He was clearly intelligent, with a quick wit and was very easy on the eye too, but it was clear from that first meeting that we were from very different backgrounds and our life experiences lead us to our first date via very different routes. This all added to the intrigue, though, and we were keen to discover just how much common ground might exist between a leather-clad biker who enjoyed head-banging heavy metal music and, as he described me, an opera-loving posh bird from Manchester. The BHG had already told me that he had a young son who stayed with him every other weekend, which I was fine with, if a little unsure as to how this might affect a possible future relationship, but if I had my reservations about this, then on our second date I was about to learn things that had the potential to rule out the possibility of a third date.

The BHG suddenly announced that he had some things to tell me that he thought I should know before we went any further and, not knowing quite what to expect, I listened carefully as he described how, many years before, he had been diagnosed with a gastric related cancer but, thankfully, it had been caught early and successfully treated. Unfortunately, the radio and chemotherapies used to treat the cancer had caused damage to his pancreas and this meant that, as a result, he was now a type 2 diabetic, which in turn had affected his heart. If all of this wasn't enough to contend with, he had a mild stroke during a routine dental procedure but, luckily, had escaped any lasting effects or disabilities.

At first, I wondered if the reason that the BHG had told me about his litany of health issues was his way of putting me off, thinking that I might perhaps have misread the signals which seemed to indicate that he was quite interested in me. The BHG was quick to assure me that it was precisely because of his very genuine interest in me that he wanted to be honest about his health from the beginning. Even if he knew that, by telling me the truth, he was taking the risk that

I might turn around and walk away, he also knew that there could be no future for us if he tried to hide it either.

I readily admit that initially, my instinct was to walk away. I have been around illness for most of my life and I was anything but sure that I had the resources to manage any ongoing issues the BHG might have in the future, even if I wanted too. But, after listening to what he had to say, my overriding feeling was one of admiration for his honesty. Far from allowing his health issues to dictate the way he lived his life, he had simply made the necessary adaptations and got on with the business of enjoying it.

Kenny had been a fit and healthy man before cancer came calling, and had never suffered a day's illness before then in his life. He died at just fifty-seven years old and my poor mother, who had never enjoyed a day of good health in hers, lived to be seventy-three, so it is clear that the state of someone's health is no measure of their longevity, my own included.

Over the course of our next few dates, it was clear that the BHG wanted to take things to the next level, which I wanted too, but found myself holding back instead. This was not because of any lingering doubts concerning his health but because, by then, I had developed a tendency to sabotage a relationship when I felt it had developed the potential to hurt me, as opposed to the meaningless flirtations I involved myself in, which had nowhere near the same capacity to do so. Inevitably, and not unreasonably, the BHG grew tired of my hot and cold behaviour and I wasn't surprised when his texts and calls dwindled down to nothing, as I made one excuse after another for not being able to see him. I did think about contacting him again after a while when I began to realise how stupid I had been, but by then I was frightened that he might have found someone else and, selfishly, this was not something I wanted to hear, so I licked my wounds and chalked it down to experience. Meanwhile, things carried on much as usual in the *Dolls House*, though my negotiations of all things DIY were not improving and my frustrations were growing.

The Dead Man's Chest and candle signs

In Jayne's hands a monkey wrench, a cordless drill or a spirit level are almost items of beauty but, in mine, they represent a very tacit threat to life and limb, so why I didn't just buy some cable ties to organise the spaghetti-like wires that protruded at all angles from behind the television, instead of purchasing a flat-pack chest of drawers to put in front of them instead, is still something of a mystery even now. I consoled myself with the fact that hundreds and thousands of people stuffing boxes into their vehicles outside Ikea every Saturday morning might indicate that you didn't need to be an expert at DIY to assemble their furniture, though Jayne did suggest that using a tin of beans to hammer in small nails was not one of my better ideas.

Having decided that I was going to tackle my project with at least a small degree of professionalism, I invested in a toolbox containing everything I thought I would need. It soon looked as though this might have been an unnecessary expense when, after poring over the assembly instructions for two hours, I remained as baffled as I had been at the outset. When I did manage to assemble the furniture, only to learn that it was upside down, at this point, I was very tempted to place the picture of the furniture – on the front of the cardboard box, in which it came – in front of the offending wires instead.

Jayne was undoubtedly right that a nine drawer chest was a bit of an ambitious first project for a DIY virgin like myself and I vowed thereafter that this foray into the world of flat-pack would be not only my first but also my last. For now, though, the wiring was hidden from sight and, on a good day, at least three of the drawers were operational – though I did have to refrain from putting my makeup bag in them when one morning I was unable to retrieve it and was forced to go out without the benefit of using its contents first. This scared the local butcher to such an extent that he immediately offered me a chair to sit on, whilst he telephoned an ambulance. Despite this, with an array of family photographs placed artfully on top of it, accompanied by three battery-operated pillar candles and a bunch of petunias, the chest of drawers did manage to look quite passable. When I sat back to admire the fruits of my labour and looked at the images of my late mother and father, Kenny, Pauline and Catherine, I christened my wonky furniture the *Dead Man's Chest* and began to insert batteries into the pillar candles, two of which flickered into life immediately, with the third stubbornly refusing to light at all. I did everything I could to try and convince the smallest of this trio of candles to light but, despite changing the batteries and jiggling the connections, it steadfastly refused to do so.

Not being the most avid of TV watchers, I am often quite happy to sit in quiet contemplation, which is exactly what I was doing one night, as I gazed at the framed faces on the *Dead Man's Chest* and wished that I could ask them for advice. I continued to flit from date to meaningless date, going nowhere fast with indecent speed. Indeed, my future was looking increasingly likely to include the acquisition of several cats, a rocking chair and an unexplained addiction to knitting stuff that nobody wants. I focused hard on a picture of Kenny, taken on our beloved Captiva Island, and pleaded with him to tell me what I could do to avoid such a fate. I can't say that I heard his voice in an audible way, or indeed the voices of any of the occupants of the *Dead Man's Chest*, but collectively I could hear them telling me very clearly to be patient and that everything would work out, just not necessarily in the way I had imagined. Whilst the receiving of this message felt very real to me, it was a bit short on detail and, not renowned for my patience, I began to question Kenny as to who, or what it might be that would bring about this satisfactory end to my current state of flux. I don't know what I expected to happen in response to my question but absolutely nothing did.

Some months later I went up to Hull to see Jayne to discuss our plans for GOWNS, something I did fairly regularly when suddenly my phone pinged to notify me of a message, which took me completely and utterly by surprise when I saw who had sent it. The last person I had been expecting to hear from was the BHG, but the butterflies fluttering around in my stomach were a testament to a mounting excitement that I had. Jayne was very patient with me during that weekend because she knew that my thoughts were elsewhere, so I left her with a promise to do better next time and returned home to a deep and meaningful conversation with the BHG, during which we both admitted to having feelings for each other. Not about to allow this chance to slip through my fingers for a second time, I promised that from now on the BHG would have my undivided attention and, whilst neither of us knew what to expect, I was now at least prepared to take the risk of being hurt in order to find out. Later, when back at home, and feeling more peaceful than I had done in a very long time, I poured myself a drink and raised my glass towards the faces on the *Dead Man's Chest* in acknowledgement of their contention that everything would *work out* just not necessarily as I had imagined. I noticed then that the smallest of the pillar candles had suddenly spluttered into life for the very first time and I sat perfectly still, almost afraid to breathe, should the fake flame peter out again. Knowing how this story might sound in the telling, I quickly took photographs of all three illuminated candles and sent them to everybody who knew that the smallest one had never worked, several of whom had even tried to fix it themselves. Even the most cynical recipient of those pictures had to admit that it was strangely coincidental that the reluctant candle had chosen that particular moment to shine and has continued to do so on-demand ever since.

Speed bumps

As in any relationship, there are tricky moments, the navigation of which will serve either to strengthen it or deal it a fatal blow and the BHG and I were not exempt from this reality. I had been married to Kenny for thirty-six years and the BHG had two marriages under his belt, as well as a long term relationship which resulted in the birth of his son. The thing about getting together with anyone later in life is that, by then, we are largely the products of our past experiences and, at our ages, they were quite extensive in number. This meant that our expectations of any new relationship were obviously heavily influenced by them and this can cause a lot to get lost in translation. For example, when the BHG moved his extensive CD collection into the *Dolls House*, he was very inclined to start packing it up again after even the most minor of disagreements, which to me seemed completely disproportionate. In my world I tend to mean what I say, say what I mean and, once having done so, will either agree to a compromise or agree to differ, and then focus on what we are having for tea. But the BHG's past experiences had taught him that any disagreement, no matter how minor, always seemed to represent the thin end of the wedge, and resulted in him having to make yet another new start from scratch. Having enjoyed one long continuous relationship without interruption, irrespective of how many rows and disagreements had punctuated it, I couldn't understand why the simplest of things could be perceived as a very real threat and it took time for the BHG to realise that not every difference of opinion would lead to a disaster. Gradually, as we began to weave our own narrative around our new and shared reality as the people we are now, we remain mindful of who, and what, we have been in the past.

The melding of two households into one is also especially interesting when at least one of you has something of a hoarding mentality. I smiled as I typed that sentence because the BHG knows that I love him for the wonderfully kind caring man that he is, and I am not given to making comparisons between him and Kenny. Despite being two very different people though, comparisons are sometimes difficult to avoid because they do share many similarities. Their love of hoarding, or should I say *collecting items of interest*, is certainly one of them. Kenny bought and sold antiques, specialising in vintage golf clubs which he bought in such quantities that they had a tendency to spill out from the two sheds outside and into the house, making cleaning the stuff of nightmares.

The worst thing that he wanted to add to his collection of objet d'art, though, was a partly fossilised corpse of a lionfish that he discovered on a beach in Sarasota. I was horrified when he suggested bringing it home and told him in no uncertain terms that, whilst his plan was probably in direct contravention of several laws, this would be the absolute least of his problems should he even think for a moment about packing a half-rotted fish inside any suitcase of mine. Reluctantly, he agreed that perhaps it was a bit of a daft idea, but then daft ideas were Kenny's stock in trade and, shortly after we arrived home and giggling like a schoolboy who had just heard the word fart for the first time, he suddenly produced the dead fish. Determined to keep possession of his latest *trophy*, he had wrapped it in a hand towel, before pouring the contents of an expensive bottle of aftershave down its mouth to help disguise the pungent odour of decaying flesh, and then concealed it amongst his hand luggage. To say that he was absolutely thrilled to have pulled off this stunt would be something of an understatement. Later, when his fascination with the fossilised fish seemed to have waned, I discreetly relocated it to our local tip.

Suffice to say that my joy at having a utility room at the *Dolls House,* in which to house the appliances that usually clutter up the kitchen, was short-lived once the BHG moved in. He is an engineer whose passions include bikes, motorbikes, along with all their various accompanying accessories and parts, and, like Jayne, he thinks tools are much more exciting than the boring inanimate objects that they appear to be to me.

For the first time in my life, my utility room gave me a place in which to hide boxes of washing powder and all those other ugly cleaning products that seem to multiply in number under the kitchen sink, but nowadays they compete for space with the BHG's ever-expanding collection of items I never even knew existed, never see used, but am assured are absolutely essential, though I did have to draw the line when I caught him trying to wash them in my dishwasher. Despite all the emotional and practical challenges of starting a new relationship in middle age, with the inevitability that the road behind is likely to be a lot longer than the one lying ahead, the rewards are without any doubt whatsoever more than worth the effort.

Third finger left hand

When the BHG proposed to me some time ago, I answered with a resounding yes – well, when I say that he asked me to marry him, I think that's what he said. He tends to speak quickly and quietly, and his dialect is a mixture of his native Lancashire and the Cornish accent he picked up during the many years he lived in the county. This means that most of the time I can't tell a word he is saying but, as he didn't object when I dragged him out to look at engagement rings, I assumed it likely that he probably had proposed. I never expected to wear another engagement ring other than the one that Kenny slipped onto my finger when I was just eighteen years old and certainly shopping for one in middle age is a very different experience.

Having spent a good few of our weekends with our noses pressed up against the windows of several jewellers, like people half our age, we were finally able to narrow our choices down to a style we both liked and began to venture inside to try some of them on. We were met by varying reactions from the counter staff, on learning that two old codgers such as ourselves wanted to purchase an actual engagement ring and their facial expressions would range, from the vaguely amused and curious, to ones of thinly disguised disgust. When this happened, I would blithely announce that I had in fact been married five times before, but I knew that this was going to be my last husband because he was so much better in bed than all the others.

When we eventually narrowed our search down to a specific ring, we set off for the jewellers one Saturday morning, hoping to make our purchase. I fully expected that the ring would need re-sizing, because of the weight I had gained, and I resolved not to be too disappointed if I couldn't bring it home with me. Whenever we go anywhere in the car the BHG will select, from his CD collection, what he likes to call *driving music* and is usually of the type that makes me want to slit my throat but, this morning, as we set off to the jewellers, his choice left me quite literally speechless.

When I was finally able to, I explained to him that Kenny, whose taste in music included mainly acoustic stuff, Country and David Bowie had surprised us all when he purchased a CD by an artist called Scooter, something that was quite a big departure from his usual preferences. He then went on to develop something of an obsession with this particular CD and would play it very loudly at every opportunity. When in the car, he had taken to winding down the window, so that people in the street would turn to see just where this music was blaring out from, only for them to witness Kenny casually leaning on his elbow, convinced that he was the epitome of cool, and not the middle-aged man having a midlife crisis that he actually was. His uncharacteristic behaviour got so bad that subversive action was the only solution so I took the CD and hid it.

Kenny searched high and low for it for days but, hidden as it was, tucked away inside the case of one of my many Welsh male voice choir CD's which he hated, he was never likely to find it. For a while there, though, it was touch and go whether or not he would simply go out and buy another copy but, never one to spend much money on himself, he decided that he'd probably had his money's worth out of the original and, thankfully, went back to listening to Kenny Rogers instead.

The story of the Scooter CD was a source of family amusement for years. Kenny never did find it and I had managed to avoid hearing it again until this morning when the BHG had chosen it for this morning's *driving music*. Ironically, this was also a big musical departure for him too and, like me, he was hearing it today for the first time in years. Sometimes fact is literally stranger than fiction and I could almost hear Kenny wishing us good luck at the jewellers, before sticking two fingers up and telling me he had finally found his Scooter CD.

Near to the jewellers is a quirky little bar, which sells the most amazing crepes with all manner of sweet and savoury fillings, which the BHG and I had grown a little too fond of and had probably contributed to the fact that we were both carrying a bit more weight than usual. In order to try and reduce our intake of them, we had resorted to calling them craps instead of crepes, a connotation with far less appeal but, as today was a special one, we decided that we would treat ourselves after we had bought the ring. When we got to the jewellers we were attended to by a lovely lady who, probably because she was nearer to our age, treated us with courtesy and respect, and we were lead to the type of comfy seats you only get to sit on when you are about to make a big purchase in somewhere like a jewellers shop.

The ring was as lovely as I remembered it and, what's more, it miraculously slipped over my knuckle with unexpected ease. As I looked at the BHG and, again, at the ring on my finger, the tears began to fall and I noticed that he too was struggling to contain his emotions but, just before we both lost it completely, he grabbed my hand and said,

"Hang on in there darling, just think about the lovely crap we'll have after this." Realising how this must

have sounded to the jeweller, we went from crying to uncontrollable giggling quicker than a Ferrari going from nought to sixty. The poor lady managed to maintain her polite professional smile throughout and, though the price of the ring was sufficiently high to have caused an involuntary bodily expulsion in anyone with a weakened constitution, I doubt she had ever had one of her clients announce so publicly that they needed to go for a crap so soon after buying one.

The BHG and I were formally engaged on New Year's Eve 2018 and celebrated with just our closest family at a small party in the *Dolls House*. It felt good to have a reason to celebrate again though when I looked at the photographs the next day, my happiness had the edge taken off it slightly when I was faced with the evidence of the true extent of my weight gain, which I had been avoiding facing up to for a long time. Faced with the prospect that the BHG might not even make it into the frame on our wedding photographs, I knew that things were now clearly out of hand and that something needed to be done.

Weighing in for a wedding

Today, there are at least six inches of snow on the ground on the driveway outside my office window, and my car is simply refusing to negotiate the steep inclines which connect our little corner of the world with roads that might just be passable. Despite having invested in a pair of heavy-duty walking boots, I still manage to skate round in them like both halves of Torvill and Dean so, for today at least, I will have to submit to the indignities of the contortions suggested on a fitness DVD. Looking on the bright side, at least the snow is preventing me from heading out to the shops and, with little food in the house, I am hoping that over the next couple of days my body will start to attack its own stores of fat for sustenance, and I will have lost half a stone and be snow-free by the weekend.

January is historically the month that people hit the gym and embark on Keto, Palaeolithic, Zone, Dukan or any other of the numerous weight loss plans out there, and I thought I would call on my fellow GOWNS, who might also be wanting to shed a few pounds, for ideas. Soon we had set up a sub-group called GREEDY GOWNS so that we can support and encourage each other, share recipe's and, in typical GOWNS style, try and have a laugh whilst we are doing it. The following is a post I wrote for GREEDY GOWNS when I realised that my current weight and the date of my wedding are not mutually compatible with finding a dress anything less than the size of a small marquee, and the best I can probably hope for now will be something akin to a two-man tent.

'Ooookay people… I might be a lot of things but have never considered myself to be delusional, after weighing myself yesterday though it turns out that I probably am something of an expert when it comes to the art of self-deception. When I first hopped onto that innocuous-looking little machine that resides in the corner of my bathroom, my first reaction was quite

favourable in that the numbers looking up at me were nowhere as bad as I feared, but that was before I found my glasses, after which I could only suspect that I might not be standing on the scales alone, or that they had malfunctioned due to lack of use over the last year, a quick check of both possibilities found no such causal effect.

Thinking that I had managed to eat reasonably well over Christmas, would suggest that the control I imagined I had exerted over my borders, was probably equivalent to the efforts made on behalf of our current government when it comes to Brexit. So today I have decided to take back control of those errant borders, and re-establish sovereignty over my eating decisions so that I can start to dispense with the useless lumps of lard that I have allowed to take over my autonomy.'

They say that patience is a virtue but, I am neither virtuous or patient, and even though my experience tells me that losing weight, especially as we age, is a process which takes much longer than it does to gain the weight in the first place, it is still a source of frustration to me, as is evident in the following post I also wrote for GREEDY GOWNS.

'Ooookay people...I really don't mind the fact that my stomach thinks my throat has been cut such is the massive reduction in the stuff going down into it. I can even cope with the constant aching of my limbs as they re-learn the art of movement but, the one thing I cannot cope with is being lied to. There is absolutely no freaking way that after all my efforts these last couple

of weeks that I have put a pound on, but that is exactly what that sodding machine in the corner of my bathroom is trying to tell me. It has got until tomorrow to tell me the truth before its new address is Weight Watchers, so it can upset some poor sod there instead. I'm actually quite gutted that it should have gone rogue on me in this way, I have just given it a year off without even looking at it much less attempting to burden it with my thunder thighs and thick ankles and this is all the thanks I get? And breathe, rant over, does anyone know if there are any calories in fresh air by any chance?'

The days and weeks are flying past with alarming speed and I am beginning to fear that the only way I will lose any significant amount of weight now, before the wedding, might have to involve the amputation of some parts of my anatomy. As I sit here and look forward to becoming a Mrs again, and in doing so, casting off a title I never wanted or asked for, I am acutely aware of just how much I have to be thankful for, and my weight issues pale into insignificance by comparison.

The final whistle

As I have alluded to several times in this book, Kenny was a lifelong Manchester United fan, though, within the context of our family, was largely on his own, in that the rest of us are supporters of what Alex Ferguson once called his *'noisy neighbours'* at Manchester City. Football was always an important part of our lives and, nowadays, as long as I promise, on the pain of death, not to engage in my usual repertoire of embarrassing goal-scoring celebrations, my insanely gifted grandsons sometimes allow me to watch them play for their local teams. It is ironic how football has provided so many parallels with my life, as it has turned out, in that it has definitely been a game of two halves and, after being stretchered off the pitch in injury time, I have returned to match fitness determined to play until the final whistle, all analogies of which I think my late husband would approve.

In order to kick off the second half of the match, the BHG and I went to choose a venue for our wedding, though we had literally no idea what we wanted, except that we wanted the day to be a celebration of how much we love each other and to share that with a small selection of those people closest to us.

 When we arrived at our chosen hotel to have a look around it, we were about to encounter yet another sign that the people on the *Dead Man's Chest* wanted to be remembered, this time in the form of Father Croft. I suddenly became aware of a voice I recognised, even though I had not heard it for many years and, as I suspected, it belonged to the very same, somewhat eccentric cleric who had presided at both the funerals of my late mother and father. I decided against starting up a conversation with Father Croft. He has likely carried out literally thousands of funerals and had no particular reason to remember me in that context. I do have vivid memories, however, of sitting in his living room at the vicarage, with my dad initially, to discuss the details of my mother's funeral and, more latterly, with my sister, when the time came to say goodbye to him too.

The chances of bumping into Father Croft when and where we did, I don't think by this point in the book you will be surprised to learn, I don't think can be adequately explained by coincidence alone. Even the date of our wedding turned out to be significant, especially as we didn't choose it ourselves. Originally, we booked with the hotel for our wedding to take place on the last weekend in October 2019, only to later learn that the registrar was unavailable that weekend and the nearest date to this that they had free was the 21st of September which, thankfully, our chosen venue was able to accommodate. It was only when I re-read what I had written about second firsts when editing this book that I realised that the new date of the 21st was somehow very appropriate.

At Kenny's funeral, my sister helped to carry his coffin into the chapel and, in September of this year, she will perform the task of giving away his now not-so-young bride to marry a man we all know would have met with his wholehearted approval. I have no doubt that my dear late husband if he could, would also want to warn the man about to become my second husband that once the ink has dried on the marriage certificate his chances of having *the last word* about anything ever again are effectively over. This realisation might be enough to cause the BHG to rise from a nice warm seat clutching a piece of paper on more than just the occasion of the ceremonial signing of the register. So, in order to prove to my late husband that I am a reformed character and, provide reassurance of this to my husband-to-be, I decided that, on this occasion, the last word will be given over to Robert Fulghum who, with the following quote, provides a perfect summation of everything I have learned concerning 'The Funny Thing About Being a Widow?'.

'I believe that imagination is stronger than knowledge. That myth is more potent than history. That dreams are more powerful than facts. That hope always triumphs over experience. That laughter is the only cure for grief. And I believe that love is stronger than death.'

The Author

Sandra E Manning is a writer, who inhabits a world that like many of us, she often struggles to make sense of. By re-framing what she sees through the prism of her humour tinted spectacles she is better able to understand, and deal with, both her own immediate environment and that which extends beyond it.

Sandra can usually be found these days, in her office in Greater Manchester writing articles for her blog or conversing with GOWNS on Facebook.

Turning her hand from writing magazine articles in the 1990's Sandra wrote The Funny Thing About Being a Widow? After the loss of her husband in 2014. There are two follow up titles in the series which are planned for release in early 2020.

You can sign up to Sandra's blog at sandraemanning.com and check out the GOWNS website @gownsgroup.co.uk

Made in the USA
Middletown, DE
21 March 2022